Ordinary People Extraordinary Royal Priests

DR. WILLIE JOUBERT

Tellwell Talent
www.tellwell.ca

ISBN
978-0-2288-3979-8 (Hardcover)
978-0-2288-3978-1 (Paperback)
978-0-2288-3980-4 (eBook)

ACKNOWLEDGEMENTS

I want to express my sincere appreciation to my wife, Eda, who dared to walk with me as we pursued a vision that took us way beyond our comfort zones. It was good to have you walk next to me as we moved through the gate to tabernacle in the wilderness.

Both of us want to thank Michael Wood for the wisdom he shared with us and for his encouragement when we "just happened to meet" in South Africa. This book is a direct result of the investment you placed in us in a short time.

I also want to acknowledge Norm for the input as we spent time in the depths of the earth!

DEDICATION

This book is dedicated to those who dare to dream big dreams and who will not hesitate to answer the call – in particular Ron Fair. We thank God for allowing us to meet you and walk with you for a season.

INTRODUCTION

Every so often, God moves in one's life in a way you never expected and could not have arranged even if you wanted. In fact, even at the time that it happens, one has no idea of the broader picture and it may take years for that to unfold.

In June 2002 we traveled from Canada to South Africa for the wedding of our youngest son who was a student at a Bible College in Cape Town. It "just so happened" that we were able to attend "The first Apostolic Summit in Africa" during this time. It also "just so happened" that God had stirred a man by the name of Michael Wood from Australia to call his friend, Andre Pelser, a few weeks prior to see how he was doing and learned about the Summit. It also "just so happened" that Michael sensed he had to be at the Summit. These divine connections set us up for a divine appointment with Michael and as we spoke with him and listened to him, many things that God had spoken to us were not only confirmed, but also ideas and concepts began to come together with greater clarity than before.

In a way it is like working on a jigsaw puzzle. The pieces started to come together and the picture began to take shape. In the process some pieces that we tried to fit in earlier, suddenly came back and now we were able to see where they could fit. One of the key pieces that suddenly fit and opened a whole new way of adding other pieces to the puzzle, had to do with a strange name – Melchizedek. We first read of him in Genesis 14 and after that there is one further reference to him in the Old Testament (Psalm 110:4) and a number of references in the New Testament, all in the letter to the Hebrews. On a personal level, about 3 years ago my wife, Eda, and I were in a local church when a visiting prophet spoke a word over us. We were never able to secure a tape to get the detail, but the one thing that we could not forget was that "we have a Melchizedek anointing". It was one of those things we sensed was important, but did not understand at the time and filed away for the future. In the meantime, we continued our journey of faith walking in ever increasing ways where we had never been before. In a very real sense, we were led to wrestle with the concepts of the structure and the foundation of the church. As we wrestled with these issues, our personal wineskins were shattered and when the dust settled, the old and comfortable church in four walls was no longer an option for us and I wrote the book "Restoring the broken foundations".

Meeting Michael was a divine appointment and when he spoke about Melchizedek, it put the next pieces of the puzzle together around this name. For me it was as if the Spirit suddenly opened my eyes to understand the letter to the Hebrews for the first time. With that the whole issue of church leadership and what we had seen and experienced just opened in a new way and confirmed what I had written in "Restoring the broken foundations."

This Book is the result of the divine appointment mentioned above and God's Spirit stirring in me to the point of explosion. It is not written to seek confrontation with many in church leadership, as we know it (although it will certainly ruffle feathers). It is written to help those within the church who wrestle with the issues find the truth, for the truth will set us, including the modern priests and Levites, free. So, if you do pick up this book or pass it on to a friend, please do not take it personally, but seek the truth for yourself in the Scriptures. As you do, remember the key words Jesus spoke to every church to which he wrote in the Book of Revelation: *"He who has an ear, let him hear what the Spirit says to the churches."*

Table of Contents

PRIESTLY ORDERS

The letter to the Hebrews as the name suggests was written primarily to Hebrew converts to Christianity. They were familiar with the Old Testament and the Aaronic order of the priesthood practiced in Judaism. The theme of this letter is the absolute supremacy of Jesus Christ as revealer and mediator of God's grace. In Christ the Aaronic order of the priesthood (Levitical priesthood) was replaced by a new order, which radically altered the existing structure of the priesthood. This new priesthood is after the order of Melchizedek of which Jesus Christ is the eternal high priest and was far superior to the old order:

> *"They (Levitical priests) serve at a sanctuary that is a copy and shadow of what is in heaven, but the ministry Jesus has received is far superior to theirs as the covenant of which he is mediator is superior to the old one and is founded on better promises."* Hebrews 8:5 -6.

We will look at these matters in detail in the chapters to follow, but it is important to set the stage here by pointing out that <u>one key issue facing the church is which order of priesthood we follow</u>. Now to some it may come as a shock, but most of the modern church structure has more in common with the Levitical priesthood than the order of Melchizedek! To put it in other words: The church's structure today is not in the order of Melchizedek as it should be, but is an Old Testament Levitical Structure with a thin veneer of Christianity. The major setback came when, with the conversion of the Roman Emperor Constantine, the church structure was changed back to a "Christianized" version of the Levitical priesthood model, combined with heathen models practiced in Roman Society and empowered by the ruling elite. The Reformation recognized some of this and in theory taught the concept of the priesthood of the believer, but in practice continued to adhere to the Levitical model.

The generally accepted division between clergy and laity in the church is totally contrary to the new covenant established by Jesus Christ and misses the very heart of the Father who designated his Son to be the high priest in the order of Melchizedek (See Hebrews 5:7-10). In fact, many in the church are no different than the recipients of the letter to the Hebrews who were slow to learn and ought to have been teachers of these truths, yet still needed someone to teach them the elementary truths (Hebrews 5:11-12). With that, let us move on to the solid food and beyond the infant diet of milk! It is much tastier to bite into the steak!

THE HOUSE OF GOD

In Hebrews 9:1 we read: *"Now the first covenant had regulations for worship and also an earthly sanctuary."* This sanctuary is then briefly described and also some of the priestly functions. We will look at these in more detail later, but first we have to focus on the structure of the sanctuary.

The first covenant was intimately linked to a physical structure. The Levitical priesthood served within this sanctuary and maintained its structure as well as the regulations for worship within the sanctuary. The first structure was portable as it was set up during the time of wandering in the desert. It was a tent with specific dimensions and partitions called the Tabernacle. Once in the Promised Land it was erected on a more permanent site at Shiloh as we read in Joshua 18:1. It may have been replaced with a more permanent structure than the tent later, but we are not sure. Sometime after that it was destroyed and Jeremiah referred to this as he prophesied that the temple of Solomon would be similarly destroyed (Jeremiah 7:12-15). Later another tabernacle was erected in Nob as we read in 1 Samuel 21. It was subsequently taken to Gibeon (See 1 Kings 3:4). Under Solomon the temple was built in Jerusalem, patterned on the Tabernacle structure and the Ark of the Covenant as well as the Tabernacle and its furnishings were stored in the temple. After the destruction of the temple by the Babylonians, it was rebuilt by the exiles that returned under Persian rule. Years later this temple was completely rebuilt by Herod the Great in an attempt to gain favor and influence within the Jewish society. This was the temple that Jesus visited and the Romans subsequently destroyed it in 70 AD.

During and after the exile another type of building arose which is known as a synagogue. The exact origin and time when these began to be built are not known, but it is safe to assume that these were built to serve as meeting places for Jews in communities where they lived, particularly as many were not able to attend or visit the temple. To this day synagogues function as meeting places and places of worship for Jewish people.

<u>Contrary to what many of us think, our faith does not require a special physical structure or building</u>. In fact, the very strength of the early church had much to do with the fact that they practiced the New Covenant understanding of the church as a Spiritual house where the lives were being built into a spiritual temple e.g. 1 Peter 2:4-5: *"As you come to him, the living stone – rejected by*

man but chosen by God and precious to him — you also like living stones are being built into a spiritual house to be a holy priesthood, offering spiritual sacrifices acceptable to God through Jesus Christ." It is interesting to note that at the dedication of the first temple as Solomon was praying, he recognized that, as the heavens could not contain God, the physical structure of the temple certainly even less! The first martyr Stephen quoted these words from Solomon just as he was about to be stoned to death (Acts 7:48-50) and so did Paul in his sermon in Athens (Acts 17:24- 25). Thus, Paul could write to the Corinthians and when discussing immorality challenge them to live a pure life, because *"your body is a temple of the Holy Spirit who is in you, whom you have received from God. You are not your own; you were bought at a price".*

Understanding this, the early church recognized the fact that they did not need a special building in order to worship and serve God. In fact, the very birth of the church took place outside in the street, when on the day of Pentecost, 120 men and women filled with the Spirit moved out of the upper room into the street and shared the message with the crowd and 3,000 were added to their group on that first day. While it was available to them as Jews, they used the temple courts for meetings — but found that they were not always welcome. Likewise, Paul as Jew started in the local synagogues of the places he visited, but within a short time he was driven out by hostile elements. This never deterred him and when needed, he rented a facility to teach as he did in Ephesus (Acts 19:9). In Acts 20:20 speaking to the elders from

Ephesus Paul remarked that he had preached and taught them publicly and from house to house. Contrary to some opinions the term "publicly" has nothing to do with a church building! It simply means wherever – whether the rented hall, the synagogue or the open air or marketplace.

For the first 300 years of the church's history, most meetings took place in local homes. We find the references all over the Book of Acts and in Paul's letters, e.g. Acts 2:46; 12:12; 16:15 and Romans 16:3-5 and 23; 1 Corinthians 16:19; Colossians 4:15 and Philemon 2. Compared to the church in our Western world the early church looked and operated very differently. It was active and grew at an exponential rate. They did not have the resources we seem to think are absolutely necessary, yet were far more effective in reaching unbelievers and changing their society. In fact, the stories in the Book of Acts, which seem to be so far removed from "our western reality" are very real today in countries like China where the church meets in homes and where church buildings are for most part non-existent.

It is important that we focus on the matter of the physical buildings we equate with the church. The Levitical priesthood (Aaronic order) was intimately linked with a physical structure set up as a holy place for the purpose of ministry. It called for a special class (or tribe) to oversee and manage the ministry and maintain the structure. Our church buildings are built in the same way to be a holy place where the people meet and receive ministry and guidance under the leadership of a special class that we call clergy. The structure is set up to emphasize the difference between the modern-day priests and Levites who manage the program and control the sanctuary and ministry and the rest of the people or laity. The front of the church building is generally higher and has specific items associated with those select individuals who serve in the offices required. Depending on the theology only certain individuals serve in some areas of the building or manage certain aspects of the programs, e.g. the pulpit is reserved for a very select group, only the designated leaders handle the sacraments, the music and songs are led by today's Levites, etc.

There is more to this: Every building (whether owned or rented) reflects a specific doctrinal belief system that separates itself from the other churches. It is often visible in the specific architecture of the building. The divisions are normally prominently displayed in the signs on the properties thus proclaiming disunity within the body of Christ to the community. The ads in the religious section of the local newspapers further emphasize the differences and divisions and are intended to draw mostly church people from another church (despite claims to the contrary). In the process we have created a consumer society approach to being the church. The need to maintain the building and programs and to support local Levites and priests and their needs means that every local church has to compete with the other churches in order to survive. Resources are spent mostly to maintain the status quo and to have a small (or large) paid staff do most of the ministry.

Once in a while we are challenged as we read Scriptures like 1 Corinthians 1:10-17 and 1 Corinthians 3 where Paul addressed the issue of divisions in the church. Let me quote a portion and paraphrase it for today: *"My brothers, some from Chloe's household have informed me that there are quarrels among you. What I mean is this: One of you says, 'I follow Paul'; another, 'I follow Apollos'; another 'I follow Cephas'; still another, 'I follow Christ.' Is Christ divided? Was Paul crucified for you? Were you baptized into Paul?"* (1 Corinthians 1:12-13). <u>Let me now paraphrase: *"I hear there are divisions among you as believers. Some claim to be Baptist. Others claim to be Presbyterians. Others say they are Spirit filled. Some say they are non-Denominational? Are we not to be one in Christ?"*</u>

As the divisions so prominently displayed in and by the buildings we call churches challenge us, the very root of the issue comes to the forefront in the way we deal with these divisions. First, we do not really want to address it! Our main focus is to rationally find reasons why it is good to have these divisions. The "answer" is found in the Old Testament and the divisions are now likened to the Israelite tribal system and we spiritualize our divisions as being e.g. "the Catholic tribe" or "the Anglican tribe". Once these divisions are spiritualized, we seek a way to display "the unity" in some public way. To do this, we gather the leading Levitical priests overseeing and managing the local temples that we call churches. As we get the pastors in one place a few times a year quoting Psalm 133, we then expect the commanded blessing! The Levitical order is very clear in this unity – for it is *like the precious oil poured on the head and running down Aaron's beard down upon the collar of his robes.* The whole focus is a hierarchical structure with the elite priesthood being the focal point. It does not matter whether we call these modern priests "spiritual gatekeepers" or "city elders" or "apostles of the city" – they will not overcome the divisions. A display of unity in the order of Levi or Aaron is not in line with the new covenant in Christ! Jesus who is the head of the church was not a priest in this order! He was declared High Priest in the order of Melchizedek and the church is the body of which he is the head. The unity of this one body is in the Spirit and it is vital to this unity to recognize that there is no division between clergy and laity! Every member is important and therefore <u>true unity begins with the breaking of the wall dividing the body into ministry professionals and laity.</u> This will become much clearer as we proceed in our study of Hebrews.

Before we move to this, we do need to look at yet one more aspect of the Levitical priesthood model that is so prominent in our modern understanding of church. As we have seen the Levitical priesthood was intimately connected with a physical structure of the sanctuary. As illustrated in the history of Israel, the building and what it represents can easily become an idolatrous object. Many a local church struggle with issues of who sits where or who may touch the organ or move what piece of furniture. Many have been driven out of the church because of these petty issues. The maintenance and cost related to the buildings and programs take a major bite out of the funds of most churches and the church doors that are closed are for the most part as a result of these costs. In terms of Biblical stewardship, the money spent on church buildings is a tremendous waste, especially when we consider the actual use of the space on a weekly basis. When we add the time and manpower spent on this it is even worse.

Closely related to these matters are the control issues proceeding from the Levitical families. Modern Levites often develop through tenure and there is evidence that like Biblical Levites genealogy can play a prominent role. Descendants of founding families are frequently Levites who control the use of the facilities or maintain the status quo when it comes to the traditions and the programs (just like we always did). In the same way there is a strong link between the music and songs and the Levitical priesthood. The choice of music and the use (or non-use) of certain instruments are more than often very important control issues in the sanctuary for those with Levitical leanings or genes. <u>No matter how we look at it, the Levitical priesthood model is one in which control and a focus on buildings and programs dominate the agenda.</u>

In sharp contrast to this we find that Jesus' model is people oriented. When e.g. he visited the synagogue, he caused concern because he healed on the Sabbath.

When he came to the temple he clashed with the leadership and cleansed the place, overturning tables and challenging the control. When he was shown the magnificent building, he prophesied that it would be demolished. Ultimately his challenge to the Levitical hierarchy that controlled the structures and programs, caused his death on the cross. But his words came true: As they destroyed his body which was the temple of the Holy Spirit, he raised it up in three days (John 2:19-22) and as he prophesied the temple in Jerusalem was destroyed to this day! Today on this third day of the Church, he is perfecting his multi membered body, the church, and he is doing this not in the Levitical order, but in the order of Melchizedek. Let us turn our focus to that.

WHO WAS MELCHIZEDEK?

Hebrews 7:1-3

"This Melchizedek was king of Salem and priest of God Most High. He met Abraham returning from the defeat of the kings and blessed him, and Abraham gave him a tenth of everything. First, his name means 'king of righteousness'; then also 'king of Salem' means 'king of peace.' Without father or mother, without genealogy, without beginning of days or end of life, like the Son of God he remains a priest forever."

The reference is to the story recorded in Genesis 14. A coalition of Canaanite kings battled another coalition, which included the kings of Sodom and Gomorrah. The latter were forced to flee and Abraham's nephew, Lot, who lived in Sodom, was taken captive. Abraham and his allies pursued the kings and routed them, rescuing Lot and recovering what was taken. As they returned, we read in Genesis 14:18-20: *"Then*

Melchizedek king of Salem brought out bread and wine. He was priest of God Most High and he blessed Abram, saying, 'Blessed be Abram by God Most High, Creator of heaven and earth. And blessed be God Most High, who delivered your enemies into your hand.' Then Abram gave him a tenth of everything."

There is nothing more about the strange figure we know as Melchizedek. He appeared in the story with no other prior references and after this we do not read anything else about him. In contrast to the Levitical priesthood with its genealogical connections to the tribal ancestor Levi, there is no genealogical record of any of Melchizedek's ancestors or of his descendants. Furthermore, he was not only a priest of God Most High, he was also the King of Salem or as it was later known, Jerusalem. His name literally means, "king of righteousness." In contrast to the Levitical priesthood, he represented a different order of priesthood – a priesthood that included royal power and authority. This was confirmed by Abraham's response to his blessing, for Abraham gave him a tenth of everything. In doing this Abraham acknowledged his royal priesthood and it also implied that Levi (a descendant still in Abraham's loins so to speak) also submitted to the Melchizedek order of priesthood as we read in Hebrews 7:4-10.

"Just think how great he was: Even the patriarch Abraham gave him a tenth of the plunder. Now the law requires the descendants of Levi who become priests to collect a tenth from the people – that is their brothers – even through their brothers are descended from Abraham. This man, however, did not trace his descent from Levi,

yet he collected a tenth from Abraham and blessed him who had the promises. And without doubt the lesser person is blessed by the greater. In one case the tenth is collected by men who die; but in the other case, by him who is declared to be living. One might even say that Levi, who collects the tenth, paid the tenth through Abraham, because when Melchizedek met Abraham, Levi was still in the body of his ancestor."

The author continues to explain that Jesus Christ is the High Priest after the order of Melchizedek. Before we get to that though, we need to look at a few more details. Within the Old Testament it was already recognized that Melchizedek represented a different order of the priesthood than Levi or his descendant Aaron. This is clear as we look at Psalm 110:

The Lord says to my Lord:
"Sit at my right hand until I make your enemies a footstool for your feet."
The Lord will extend your mighty scepter from Zion;
You will rule in the midst of your enemies.

Your troops will be willing on your day of battle.
Arrayed in holy majesty, from the womb of the
dawn you will receive the dew from your youth.

The Lord has sworn and will not change his mind:
"You are a priest forever, in the order of Melchizedek."

The Lord is at your right hand; he will crush kings on the day of his wrath. He will judge the nations, heaping up the dead and crushing the rulers of the whole earth.

He will drink from a brook beside the way;
therefore he will lift up his head.

This Davidic Psalm had a messianic theme and Jesus picked it up in his question to the Pharisees as recorded in Matthew 22:41-46. The point Jesus made was that the Messiah was not just a descendant of David, but was also David's Lord. The royal authority of the Messiah was from eternity as he was not just the son of David, but also the Son of God. At the same time the Messiah was not only king, but was declared to be a priest forever in the order of Melchizedek. On the day of Pentecost, the apostle Peter raised this in his message by quoting this Psalm to prove that Jesus was indeed the expected Messiah (Acts 2:34-36).

Putting these together, we see that the Levitical priesthood was very different from the order of Melchizedek. The order of Melchizedek was an eternal order. The Levitical priesthood was for a season. The Aaronic order was linked to one tribe and determined by human genealogy. The order of Melchizedek was not dependent on genealogical lineage. The order of Melchizedek brought the Aaronic order to an end and radically transformed priestly ministry.

The reason for this paradigm shift is given in Hebrews 7:11-22. Let us read this:

If perfection could have been attained through the Levitical priesthood (for on the basis of it the law was given to the people), why was there still need for another priest to come — one in the order of Melchizedek, not in the order of Aaron? For when there is a change of the priesthood, there must also be a change of the law. He of whom these things are said belonged to a different tribe, and no one from that tribe has ever served at the altar. For it is clear that our Lord descended from Judah, and in regard to that tribe Moses said nothing about priests. And what we have said is even more clear if another priest like Melchizedek appears, one who has become a priest not on the basis of a regulation as to his ancestry but on the basis of an indestructible life. For it is declared:

"You are priest forever, in the order of Melchizedek."

The former regulation is set aside because it was weak and useless (for the law made nothing perfect), and a better hope is introduced, by which we draw near to God.

And it was not without an oath! Others became priests without any oath, but he became a priest with an oath when God said to him:

"The Lord has sworn, and will not change his mind:

'You are a priest forever.'"

Because of this oath, Jesus has become the guarantor of a better covenant.

The old covenant with its laws and regulations was not perfect and did not produce perfection. The Levitical priesthood did not meet the needs and was therefore imperfect. As a result, there was recognition even in the Old Testament that a new order of priesthood was to come in the future. This was spoken forth by David in Psalm 110, which is quoted by the author in this passage.

In the person and work of Jesus Christ this new order became a reality. The change of priesthood is very clear as Jesus was not from the tribe of Levi and could thus not serve in the Aaronic order of the priesthood. In Christ the former regulation regarding the priesthood is set aside (verse 18) and a new and perfect eternal order is introduced. The eternal character of this change is underlined by the fact that God swore an oath when Jesus was declared to be priest forever in the order of Melchizedek. Not only that, as we continue, we see that Jesus became the eternal High Priest in the order of Melchizedek. Let us continue and look more closely at Jesus in this role.

JESUS CHRIST AS HIGH PRIEST

*T*he main difference between the two orders of priesthood centers on the High Priests of each order. Hebrews 5:1-4 describes the selection and appointment of the Levitical High Priest in the following words:

Every High Priest is selected from among men and is appointed to represent them in matters related to God, to offer gifts and sacrifices for sins. He is able to deal gently with those who are ignorant and are going astray, since he himself is subject to weakness. <u>This is why he has to offer sacrifices for his own sins</u>, as well as for the sins of the people. No one takes this honor upon himself; he must be called by God just as Aaron was."

It is very important to note that the Levitical High Priest did not merely offer sacrifices for the sins of the people, but also for his own sins. This is again stressed in Hebrews 7:27. However, our High Priest in the order of Melchizedek, is very different in this respect as we read in Hebrews 4:14-15:

> *Therefore, since we have a great High Priest who has gone through the heavens, Jesus the Son of God, let us hold firmly to the faith we profess. For we do not have a High Priest who is unable to sympathize with our weaknesses, but we have one who has been tempted in every way, just as we are — <u>yet was without sin.</u> Let us then approach the throne of grace with confidence, so that we may receive mercy and find grace to help us in our time of need.*

But there is another major difference that we need to see: The Levitical priests including the Aaronic High Priest were regularly replaced as they died. Each High Priest in this order only served in office for a period of time. Thus, there have been many that served in the office that began with Aaron. In light of this and what we noticed above, we read:

> *Now there have been many of those priests, since death prevented them from continuing in office; <u>but because Jesus lives forever, he has a permanent priesthood.</u> Therefore, he is able to save completely those who come to God through him, because he always lives to intercede for them.* Hebrews 7:23-25.

The order of Melchizedek is from eternity to eternity, but the Aaronic order was only for a brief season in time. This is very clear as we turn to the first chapter of the letter where the author summarizes the superior position of Jesus Christ in these words:

In the past God spoke to our fathers through the prophets at many times and in various ways, but in these last days he has spoken to us by his Son, whom he appointed heir of all things and through whom he made the universe. The Son is the radiance of God's glory and the exact representation of his being, sustaining all things through his powerful word. After he had provided purification for sins, he sat down at the right hand of the Majesty in heaven. So he became as much superior to the angels as the name he has inherited is superior to theirs. Hebrews 1:1-4.

Following this the author continues to explain the superior position of Jesus quoting from various Scriptures. The point to note is that our High Priest in the order of Melchizedek was before creation and thus from eternity and to eternity. This why we read: *"This Melchizedek was king of Salem. Without father or mother, without genealogy, without beginning of days or end of life, like the Son of God he remains priest forever."* Hebrews 7:1 and 3.

The good news of Jesus Christ is that this eternal Son of God came to the earth to become one of us and to open the door to eternity for us. In the process he was affirmed as High Priest in the eternal order of Melchizedek by the Father and opened the door for us to become *a chosen people, a royal priesthood, a holy nation, a people belonging to God, so that we may declare the praises of who called us out of darkness into his wonderful light* (See 1 Peter 2:9). We will look at this in more detail later, but it is of the utmost importance to note that <u>*in Christ we are a kingdom of priests in the eternal order of Melchizedek.*</u> In him our earthly genealogy and our human past are radically changed through a new birth and we are appointed to the ministry for which we were ordained from before the foundation of the earth. This holds very important consequences for the church and its ministry.

However, before we move to these matters, we have to look at Jesus' ministry as High Priest for us.

JESUS' MINISTRY ON EARTH AS HIGH PRIEST

In Hebrews 9 the author laid the foundations to understand the ministry of Jesus as High Priest in the order of Melchizedek. In verses 1-5 he described the earthly sanctuary and its furnishings used for worship according to the regulations of the first covenant. Then we read:

> *When everything had been arranged like this, the priests entered regularly into the outer room to carry on their ministry. But only the High Priest entered the inner room, and that only once a year, and never without blood, which he offered for himself and for the sins the people had committed in ignorance. The Holy Spirit was showing that the way into the Most Holy Place had not yet been disclosed as long as the first tabernacle was still standing. This is an illustration for the present time, indicating that the gifts and sacrifices*

being offered were not able to clear the conscience of the worshiper. They are only a matter of food and drink and various ceremonial washings – external regulations applying until the time of the new order. Hebrews 9:6-10.

Under the Levitical priesthood, only the High Priest was able to enter into the Most Holy Place and that only once a year on the Day of Atonement. A thick curtain closed the Most Holy Place off from the rest of the sanctuary and no person except the High Priest had access to the inner sanctuary. The Aaronic order of the priesthood could not provide a way into the very presence of God for the people and the curtain shut that out! <u>At this point it is extremely important to note that the way into the Most Holy Place had not yet been disclosed as long as the first tabernacle was still standing.</u> Worship in the earthly sanctuary including the actions of the Aaronic High Priest on the Day of Atonement did not provide the way into the Most Holy Place. In fact, the endless repetition of the sacrifices proved that these regulations could not open the way and simply served as illustrations for the future. Listen how Hebrews 10:1-4 puts it:

The law is only a shadow of the good things that are coming – not the realities themselves. For this reason, it can never, by the same sacrifices repeated endlessly year after year, make perfect those who draw near to worship. If it could, would they not have stopped being offered? For the worshipers would have been cleansed once for all, and would no longer have felt guilty for their sins. But those sacrifices are an annual reminder of sins, because it is impossible for the blood of bulls and goats to take away sins.

Now the good news is this: What the Aaronic order of priesthood could not do was done by the new order called the order of Melchizedek! This is the very essence of the message confirmed in the letter to the Hebrews as we read e.g. in Chapter 9:11-15:

> *When Christ came as High Priest of the good things that are already here, he went through the greater and more perfect tabernacle that is not man-made, that is to say, not a part of this creation He did not enter by the blood of goats and calves, but he entered the Most Holy Place once for all by his own blood, having obtained eternal redemption. The blood of goats and bulls and the ashes of a heifer sprinkled on those who are ceremonially unclean sanctify them so that they are outwardly clean. How much more than will the blood of Christ, who through the eternal Spirit offered himself unblemished to God, cleanse our consciences from acts that lead to death, so that we may serve the living God! For this reason, Christ is the mediator of a new covenant that those who are called may receive the promised eternal inheritance – now that he has died as a ransom to set them free from the sins committed under the first covenant.*

Before we continue with this theme, let us pause for a moment and allow me to again raise a key issue about our current church structures. Earlier I stated that much of the church has never truly wrestled with the implications of the priesthood of the believer. As a result, almost all in the Western world think of church as a building and programs overseen by professional clergy. In doing this we have moved away from the order of Melchizedek and created a Christianized version of the Aaronic order. We do accept Jesus as High Priest, but have instituted a Levitical hierarchy that functions as mediator to our Mediator for many in the church. Therefore, many come to get ministry at the altar and they repeat that year after year with little change and in the eyes of many only "the Pastor" can really pray effectively or visit the sick! We have created man-made sanctuaries where year after year we endlessly repeat the cycle e.g. summer VBS followed by the "Back to Church and Sunday school routine"; Christmas programs and the break after Christmas; then the lead up to Easter followed by the gradual wind-down of the program and the Sunday school closing and on and on. Is it really that different from the picture presented in Hebrews 10? <u>I want to challenge you to keep these things in mind as we continue to look at the work and ministry of Jesus, our High Priest in the order of Melchizedek.</u>

Let us read further in Hebrews 9:24-28:

> *For Christ did not enter a manmade sanctuary that was only a copy of the true one; he entered heaven itself, now to appear for us in God's presence. Nor did he enter to offer himself again and again, the way the High Priest enters the Most Holy Place every year with blood that is not his own. Then Christ would have had to suffer many times since the creation of the world. But now he has appeared once for all at the end of the ages to do away with sin by the sacrifice of himself. Just as man is destined to die once, and after that to face judgment, so Christ was sacrificed once to take a way the sins of many people; and he will appear a second time to bring salvation to those who are waiting for him.*

On Good Friday Jesus Christ died on a cross on a hill called Golgotha. The High Priest in the order of Melchizedek offered his own life as a perfect sacrifice. *God made him who had no sin to be sin for us, so that in him we might become the righteousness of God.* (2 Corinthians 5:21). When he entered heaven itself and into the very presence of God, he entered with blood that was his own and shed for the forgiveness of the sins of the world. Once and for all he dealt with sin. In this he opened the way for us, having been declared righteous through his sacrifice, to enter into the same presence of God. This is why the curtain separating the Most Holy Place from the rest of the temple was torn in two from top to bottom as Matthew said in Matthew 27:51. <u>At that very moment it signaled the end of the Aaronic order of the priesthood and the revelation of the new order of Melchizedek. His suffering and death on earth opened the door for us to have a permanent access into the very presence of God and because of that he was designated as High Priest in the new order as we read in Hebrews 5:7 -10:</u>

> *During the days of Jesus' life on earth, he offered up prayers and petitions with loud cries and tears to the one who could save him from death, and he was heard because of his reverent submission. Although he was a son, he learned obedience from what he suffered and, once made perfect, he became the source of eternal salvation for all who obey him and was designated by God to be High Priest in the order of Melchizedek.*

To understand Jesus' ministry in context, we need to return to the opening chapters of this letter. As we saw earlier, Hebrews 1 described the superior position of Jesus as eternal Son of God through whom the universe was created. He is far superior to the angels. They are spirits sent to serve those who will inherit the salvation that Jesus Christ made possible, who become the members of his body, the church. (See Hebrews 1:14). Chapter 2 then turns the focus on this salvation that was accomplished for us in Christ and confirmed by those who witnessed the life, death and resurrection of our Lord and affirmed by God in the birth of the church. We are urged to pay careful attention to this as we read in Hebrews 2:1-4:

> *We must pay more careful attention to what we have heard, so that we do not drift away. For if the message spoken by angels was binding and every violation and disobedience received its just punishment, how shall we escape if we ignore such a great salvation? This salvation, which was first announced by the Lord, was confirmed to us by signs, wonders and various miracles, and gifts of the Holy Spirit distributed according to his will.*

Let us now turn our attention on what our High Priest in the order of Melchizedek gained for us through his obedience and suffering.

HEIRS OF THE PROMISE

The opening chapters of Scripture tell the story of creation and of the fall of mankind. The creator of the universe through the power of his creative word spoke the universe into being and in the same way created life on this planet. Then he took the soil of this world and in his hands it was molded into human beings in which he breathed the life of his Spirit. Then God blessed them and gave them authority over the earth and its creatures, to rule and reign, and he walked in intimacy with them. Through disobedience they chose to eat from the tree of the knowledge of good and evil and as a result Satan and his host were given power and authority. Mankind then lived under the curse and fear of death and the access to the garden where they experienced the intimacy with God was closed. In the midst of this darkness there was the light of a promise of one *"who would crush the head of the serpent even as the serpent strike his heel."* Genesis 3:15.

Many years later God called Abram and sent him from Mesopotamia to the Promised Land. In obedience and faith, he went with Sarah and in their old age against all odds they had a miracle baby that they called Isaac. With every promise tied to this boy, Abraham was put to the test and God told him to sacrifice his only son whom he loved. Again, Abraham acted in obedience and at the last minute God stopped him and supplied a substitute in the form of a ram (Genesis 15-22). Then we read these words in Genesis 22:15-18:

> *The angel of the Lord called Abraham from heaven a second time and said, "I swear by myself, declares the Lord, that because you have done this and have not withheld your son, I will surely bless you and make your descendants as numerous as the stars in the sky and as the sand on the seashore. Your descendants will take possession of the cities of their enemies, <u>and through your offspring all nations on earth will be blessed, because you have obeyed me."</u>*

This very act of Abraham became a symbol of God's grace, for he sent his Son from heaven to earth to be born a descendant of Abraham. Like Abraham who did not hold back his son, the God of heaven did not hold back his Son, but sent him to be sacrificed on a cross. This Son who was declared to be eternal High Priest in the order of Melchizedek *took up our infirmities and carried our sorrows, yet we considered him stricken by God, smitten by him, and afflicted. He was pierced for our iniquities.*

The punishment that brought us peace was upon him and by his wounds we are healed (Isaiah 53:4-5). In the process the promises to Abraham became available to us through Jesus as Paul wrote in Galatians 3:26-4:7:

> *You are all sons of God through faith in Christ Jesus, for all of you who were baptized into Christ have clothed yourself with Christ. There is neither Jew nor Greek, slave nor free, male nor female, for you are all one in Christ Jesus. If you belong to Christ, then you are Abraham's seed, and heirs according to the promise.*
>
> *What I am saying is that as long as the heir is a child, he is no different from a slave, although he owns the estate. He is subject to guardians and trustees until the time set by his father. So also, when we were children we were in slavery under the basic principles of the world. But when the time had fully come, God sent his Son, born of a woman, born under law to redeem those under the law, so that we might receive the full rights of sons. Because you are sons, God sent the Spirit of his Son into our hearts, the Spirit who calls out, "Abba, Father." So you are no longer a slave, but a son; and since you are a son, God has made you also an heir.*

Now it is very interesting to note that Paul was writing to the Galatians and they had begun to drift away from the freedom in Christ to legal bondage again. They were again slipping away from the order of Melchizedek into the order of Aaron with its rules and regulations, in particular the circumcision (see Galatians 5:1-16). This is very similar to the challenge that faced the Hebrew believers to whom our author wrote and that is the reason why he warned them not to drift away from the salvation they received (see Hebrews 2:1). This salvation opened the door for us to receive the promise to Abraham – but it is connected with the order of Melchizedek as we read in Hebrews 6:13-20:

> *When God made his promise to Abraham, since there was no one greater for him to swear by, he swore by himself, saying, "I will surely bless you and give you many descendants." And so, after waiting patiently, Abraham received what was promised.*

> *Men swear by someone greater than themselves, and the oath confirms what is said and puts an end to all argument. Because God wanted to make the unchanging nature of his purpose very clear to the heirs of what was promised, he confirmed it with an oath. God did this so that, by two unchangeable things in which it is impossible for God to lie, we who have fled to take hold of this hope offered to us may be greatly encouraged. We have this hope as an anchor for the soul, firm and secure. <u>It enters the inner sanctuary behind the curtain, where Jesus, who went before us, has entered on our behalf. He has become a High Priest forever, in the order of Melchizedek.</u>*

As we put these things together, we discover an incredible picture. When Jesus died, the curtain in the earthly sanctuary was torn from top to bottom, which means that God himself tore it apart. Now this earthly sanctuary is a copy and shadow of what is in heaven for we read in Hebrews 8:5: *They serve at a sanctuary that is a copy and shadow of what is in heaven. This is why Moses was warned when he was about to build the tabernacle: "See to it that you make everything according to the pattern shown you on the mountain.*" Therefore, when God tore the curtain in two, it symbolized two things: First it meant that the Aaronic order and its regulations were replaced by the new order of Melchizedek. Second it symbolized that just as the access to the Most Holy Place in the earthly sanctuary was no longer closed, so there was a way open to the believer to enter into the true tabernacle. Let us follow this with our author, beginning with Hebrews 8:1- 2:

> *The point of what we are saying is this: We do have such a High Priest, who sat down at the right hand of the Majesty in heaven, and who serves in the sanctuary, the true tabernacle set up by the Lord, not by man.*

This is explained in more detail in the next chapter where we read:

> *When Christ came as High Priest of the good things that are already here, he went through the greater and more perfect tabernacle that is not man-made, that is to say not part of this creation. He did not enter by the blood of goats and calves; but he entered the Most Holy Place once for all by his own blood, having obtained eternal redemption.* Hebrews 9:11 -12.

> *For this reason, Christ is the mediator of a new covenant, that those who are called may receive the promised eternal inheritance* – *now that he has died as a ransom to set them free from the sins committed under the first covenant.* Hebrews 9:15.

> *For Christ did not enter a man-made sanctuary that was only a copy of the true one; he entered heaven itself, now to appear for us in God's presence.* Hebrews 9:24.

In the earthly sanctuary the Aaronic High Priest entered the Most Holy Place once a year to fulfil the regulations for the Day of Atonement. When finished he came back and the curtain remained closed so that the access to the inner sanctuary was not open to anyone else but him. As we have seen the Aaronic regulations and sacrifices could not cleanse the people and they had to do this repeatedly (see Hebrews 10:1-4). However, Jesus came in submission to the will of God the Father and walked the way of obedience even to death on the cross (see Philippians 2:6-8). His obedience in submission to the Father is described as follows in Hebrews 5:7-10:

> *During the days of Jesus' life on earth, he offered up prayers and petitions with loud cries and tears to the one who could save him from death, and he was heard because of his reverent submission. Although he was a son, he learnt obedience from what he suffered and, once made perfect, he became the source of eternal salvation for all who obey him and was designated by God to be the High Priest in the order of Melchizedek.*

He came to offer himself as a perfect sacrifice. The first Adam closed the door to the intimacy and to the full presence of God through disobedience, but the second Adam walked in submission and learned obedience through his suffering. In fact, he came knowing that the price needed to end the Aaronic priesthood and to establish the new order of Melchizedek would be his suffering and death on the cross as our author says in Hebrews 10:5-10:

Therefore, when Christ came into the world, he said:

"Sacrifice and offering you did not desire, but a body you prepared for me; with burnt offerings and sin offering you were not pleased. Then I said, 'Here I am – it is written about me in the scroll – I have come to do your will, O God.'"

First, he said, "Sacrifices and offerings, burnt offerings and sin offerings you did not desire, nor were you pleased with them" (although the law required them to be made). Then he said, "Here I am, I have come to do your will." He sets aside the first to establish the second. <u>And by that will we have been made holy through the sacrifice of the body of Jesus once and for all.</u>

Through Jesus we have been cleansed once and for all and made holy. In one day, the old order was replaced by the new order and it became obsolete. In the process a new holy nation, a kingdom of priests in the order of Melchizedek was created and we were given confidence to boldly enter into the Most Holy Place. Listen to Hebrews 10:11-23:

Day after day every priest stands and performs his religious duties; again and again he offers the same sacrifices, which can never take away sins. <u>But when this priest had offered for all time one sacrifice for sins, he sat down at the right hand of God.</u> Since that time, he waits for his enemies to be made his footstool, because <u>by one sacrifice he has made perfect forever those who are being made holy.</u>

<u>The Holy Spirit also testifies to us about this. First, he says:</u>

"This is my covenant I will make with them after that time, says the Lord. I will put my laws in their hearts and I will write them on their minds."

Then he adds:

'Their sins and lawless acts I will remember no more.'

And where these have been forgiven, there is no longer any sacrifice for sin.

Therefore, brothers, since we have confidence to enter the Most Holy Place by the blood of Jesus, by a new and living way opened for us through the curtain, that is, his body, and since we have a great Priest over the house of God, let us draw near with a sincere heart in full assurance of faith, having our hearts sprinkled to cleanse us from a guilty conscience and having our bodies washed with pure water. Let us hold unswervingly to the hope we profess, for he who promised is faithful.

Let us stop for a moment and get the picture in perspective: In Christ the old order with a Levitical hierarchy of priests managing and directing worship and ministry on behalf of the people became totally obsolete. In Christ we were cleansed to be holy and righteous so that every believer can enter boldly into the Most Holy Place. On the day of Pentecost, the risen Lord poured out his Spirit on all in the upper room — not just on the twelve apostles! When Peter spoke to the crowd in the street, he quoted from the prophecy of Joel saying, *"In the last days, God says, I will pour out my Spirit on all people. Your sons and daughters will prophesy, your young men will see visions; your old men will dream dreams. Even on my servants, both men and women, I will pour out my Spirit in those days, and they will prophesy."* (See Acts 2:17-18). As the message spread, ordinary people were filled with the Spirit and did the work of ministry. They did not build buildings and needed no professional clergy to oversee the people, buildings and programs. That was part of the old and now obsolete Aaronic order and they did not need to follow that any more. Those who were leaders earned the right to their leadership by building relationships as they served in humility – not because they had a title like "Pastor" or "Reverend."

In Christ the new order of Melchizedek replaced the old order and with that the eternal destiny of each believer was being restored. Ordinary people were transformed by the presence and power of the Spirit and they began to change the world in which they live seeing what cannot be seen and overcoming the enemy through the power of the cross. It is to this that we need to turn our attention next.

THE OLD HAS GONE THE NEW HAS COME

In 1 Corinthians 5:14-17 we read:

For Christ's love compels us, because we are convinced that one died for all, and therefore all died. And he died for all that those who live should no longer live for themselves but for him who died for them and was raised again.

So, from now on we regard no one from a worldly point of view. Though we once regarded Christ in this way, we do so no longer. <u>Therefore, if anyone is in Christ, he is a new creation; the old has gone, the new has come!</u>

*L*et us consider the above in the light of what we learned about Jesus as our High Priest in the order of Melchizedek. We have noticed that one of the differences between the order of Melchizedek and the Aaronic order of the priesthood centered around the fact that the latter was based on genealogy and the former not. The Aaronic priests were descended from the patriarch Levi and followed one another along family lines. In contrast, the author of Hebrews wrote, *"without father or mother, without genealogy, without beginning of days or end of life, like the Son of God Melchizedek remains a priest forever."* Hebrews 7:3.

As believers we have little difficulty accepting the eternal aspects of the life of Jesus. When we read: *"In the beginning was the Word, and the Word was with God and the Word was God. He was with God in the beginning. Through him all things were made; without him nothing was made that has been made"* (John 1:1-3), we have no trouble relating that to Jesus that came in the flesh. In the same way we read 1 Peter 1:18-20:

> *For you know that it was not with perishable things such as silver or gold that you were redeemed from the empty way of life handed down to you from your forefathers, <u>but with the precious blood of Christ, a lamb without blemish or defect. He was chosen before the creation of the world, but was revealed in these last times for your sake.</u>*

Further John related the vision of the risen Lord in Revelation 1 and we read how Jesus says: *"Do not be afraid. I am the First and the Last. I am the Living One; I was dead and behold I am alive for ever and ever! And I hold the keys of death and Hades."* (Revelation 1:17-18). Our High Priest in the order of Melchizedek is indeed a priest without beginning of days or end of life as we read in Hebrews 7:3.

Likewise, we have little difficulty accepting eternity as future for both believers and unbelievers (whether in heaven or hell). We all know John 3:16 by heart: *"For God so loved the world that he gave his only begotten Son that whoever believes in him shall not perish, but have eternal life."* We know the story of Lazarus and again most believers can quote Jesus' words to Martha from memory: *"I am the resurrection and the life. He who believes in me will live, even though he dies; and whoever lives and believes in me will never die."* John 11:25.

Thus, we understand that *in Christ* we receive an eternal inheritance. As we saw above, the old is gone and the new has come (2 Corinthians 5:17). However, there is more to this than merely being set free from the past through the forgiveness of sin. The order of Melchizedek into which we are incorporated is an order that restores and redirects our lives *by restoring the divine purpose of God for our lives from before creation!*

Let us begin by reading Ephesians 1:1-14:

> *Praise be to the God and Father of our Lord Jesus Christ, who has blessed us in the heavenly realms with every spiritual blessing in Christ. For he chose us in him before the creation of the world to be holy and blameless in his sight. In love he predestined us to be adopted as his sons through Jesus Christ, in accordance with his pleasure and will - to the praise of his glorious grace, which he has freely given us in the One he loves. In him we have redemption through his blood, the forgiveness of sins, in accordance with the riches of God's grace that he lavished on us with all wisdom and understanding. And he made known to us the mystery of his will according to*

his good pleasure, which he purposed in Christ, to be put into effect when the times will have reached their fulfillment - to bring all things in heaven and on earth together under one head, even Jesus.

In him we were also chosen, having been predestined according to the plan of him who works out everything in conformity with the purpose of his will, in order that we, who were the first to hope in Christ, might be for the praise of his glory. And you also were included in Christ when you heard the word of truth, the gospel of salvation. Having believed you were marked in him with a seal, the promised Holy Spirit, who is a deposit guaranteeing our inheritance until the redemption of those who are God's possession — to the praise of his glory.

Therefore, in Christ we receive not only the promise of the present and future, but there is a restoration of the purposes of God for our lives ordained before creation. God is fully able to redeem the past! Every person on this planet is here by the divine purpose of God, as David wrote in Psalm 139:13-16:

For you created my inmost being;

you knit me together in my mother's womb.

I praise you for I am fearfully and wonderfully made;

your works are wonderful, I know that full well.

My frame was not hidden from you when I was made in the secret place.

When I was woven together in the depths of the earth, your eyes saw my unformed body.

All the days ordained for me were written in your book.

Even though Satan succeeded in causing the fall of mankind, God is more than able to turn the evil to good through his divine plan and purpose. This is nowhere more clearly illustrated than in the cross where while *we were dead in our sins and in the uncircumcision of our sinful nature, God made us alive with Christ. He cancelled the written code with its regulations that was against us and that stood opposed to us; he took it away nailing it to the cross. And having disarmed the powers and authorities, he made a public spectacle of them, triumphing over them by the cross.* Colossians 2:13-15.

In Christ every human life on this earth can be turned around to fully accomplish God's divine purpose. Through disobedience, humanity lost the relationship with God as our Father. We became dead in our sins and no longer knew how to relate to God. We became spiritual orphans who did not know how to say "Abba, Father." But in Christ we met the Father, for he came to make him known as we read in John 1:18:

No one has ever seen God, but God the One and Only, who is at the Father's side, has made him known.

When we receive the Holy Spirit, we receive the Spirit of sonship. *And by him we cry, "Abba, Father."* In the process we are being restored to our eternal origin and the very purpose for our lives on earth and into eternity.

In Christ we are brought into the eternal order of Melchizedek to be a kingdom of priests fulfilling our divine destiny ordained before creation itself. Listen how Paul expressed this in Ephesians 2:10:

> *For we are God's workmanship, created in Christ Jesus to do good works, which God prepared in advance for us to do.*

The great tragedy of the Church is that so many have chosen the Levitical model of the priesthood. Millions who are brought to faith settle for inactivity in the pew or chair and pay the professionals to "be priests" for them. The other side of this coin is that the modern Aaronic priests and their Levitical helpers cater to the consumer needs of the members and in turn use them to fund the programs and buildings in the name of God. The vast majority of churchgoers in the Western world fall in this trap and most have no idea that they were called before creation to serve in the order of Melchizedek. Most of the membership of the church has no idea that they are created as spiritual beings from eternity and that they can have intimate fellowship with God the Father. Many who do know that they have been called and ordained to fulfil a divine plan miss the opportunity, because they are submitted and choose to be submitted to insecure Aaronic leaders who would not release them. They do not know that they need no human permission to do God's work and if they were to step out in obedience, they will find others to help them in areas of encouragement, accountability and support. Most believers are tied and imprisoned by the modern Aaronic traditions and the earthly sanctuary with its

Sunday ritual. This is nothing less than having the torn veil sewn together again to support the Levitical priesthood by legitimizing the need for an earthly caste of priests to serve at the altar and enter on their behalf into the Most Holy Presence.

But it is time for us to move on and consider the ministry that we have been called to do and the power and authority we have in Christ.

MAKING KNOWN THE MANIFEST WISDOM OF GOD

The apostle Paul wrote about the revelation of the mystery that made him a missionary to the Gentiles in Ephesians 3:4-13. Let us read this to set the stage for understanding the ministry to which we are called.

In reading this, then, you will be able to understand my insight into the mystery of Christ, which was not made known to men in other generations as it has now been revealed by the Spirit to God's holy apostles and prophets. This mystery is that through the gospel the Gentiles are heirs together with Israel, members together of one body, and sharers together in the promise of Christ Jesus.

I became a servant of this gospel by the gift of God's grace given me through the working of his power. Although I am less than the least of all God's people, this grace was given me: to preach to the

Gentiles the unsearchable riches of Christ, and to make plain to everyone the administration of this mystery, which for ages past was kept hidden in God, who created all things. <u>His intent was that now, through the church, the manifold wisdom of God should be made known to the rulers and authorities in the heavenly realms, according to his eternal purpose which he accomplished in Christ Jesus our Lord.</u> In him and through faith in him we may approach God with freedom and confidence. I ask you therefore, not to be discouraged because of our sufferings for you, which are your glory.

The apostle says that God accomplished his eternal purpose in Christ Jesus. In and through him we have been given access to God with no restrictions, because we have been forgiven. As eternal High Priest in the order of Melchizedek he opened the way once and for all and in God's grace we, as Gentiles, were included and share in the very promises to Abraham as co-heirs with Christ (see Romans 8:16-17). Now the ultimate purpose of God in Christ is wonderfully described in 1 Corinthians 15:22-28 where Paul speaks about the restoration of what was lost in Adam through the fall in these words:

For as in Adam all die, so <u>in Christ all will be made alive.</u> But each in his own turn: Christ, the first fruits; then, when he comes, those who belong to him. <u>Then he hands over the kingdom to God the Father after he has destroyed all dominion, authority and power. For he must reign until he has put all his enemies under his feet.</u> The last enemy to be destroyed is death. For he "has put everything under his feet." Now, when it says that "everything" has been put under him, *it is clear that this does not include God himself, who put everything under Christ. <u>When he has done this, then the Son himself will be made subject to him who put everything under him, so that God will be all and in all.</u>*

The ultimate purpose of God is that all of creation will be under the submission of his Son, the High Priest, who will then hand it to the Father so that God will be all and in all. The victory that was won on the cross will become all-encompassing and the very schemes of the Devil will be completely reversed. In order for this to take place God sent his Son and when he paid the price for our redemption, he was raised and seated at the right hand of God in the heavenly realms where he has the ultimate authority. At the same time God made him the head of his body, the church, and empowered us corporately with the same power used to raise Jesus to this position. Paul's prayer in Ephesians 1:17-23 was that we might grasp this revelation:

I keep asking that the God and Father of our Lord Jesus Christ, the glorious Father, may give you the Spirit of wisdom and revelation, so that you may know him better. I pray also that the eyes of your heart may be enlightened in order that you may know the hope to which he has called you, the riches of his glorious inheritance in the saints, and his incomparably great power for us who believe. That power is like the working of his mighty strength, which he exerted in Christ when he raised him from the dead and seated him at his right hand in the heavenly realms, far above all rule and authority, power and dominion, and above every title that can be given in the present age but also in the one to come. And God placed all things under his feet and appointed him to be head over everything for the church, which is his body, the fullness of him who fills everything in every way.

Paul then continues by saying that as co-heirs with Jesus we were also raised with him and seated in heavenly realms, empowered and commissioned to overcome every opposition to the divine purpose:

And God raised us up with Christ and seated us with him in the heavenly realms in Christ Jesus, in order that in the coming ages he might show the incomparable riches of his grace expressed in his kindness to us in Christ Jesus. (Ephesians 2:6).

What is absolutely amazing is that in God's divine purpose he gave us as humans such a prominent place and role. In fact, let us turn to Hebrews once more and this time to the second chapter. Having warned the readers not take salvation, which was revealed in Christ and confirmed by the power of the Spirit in the church lightly, the author then said:

It is not to angels that God has subjected the world to come, about which we are speaking. But there is a place where someone has testified:

"What is man that you are mindful of him,

the son of man that you care for him?

You made him a little lower than the angels;

you crowned him with glory and honor.

In putting everything under him, God left nothing that was not subject to him. Yet at present we do not see everything subject to him. But we see Jesus, who was made a little lower than the angels, now crowned with glory and honor because he suffered death, so that by the grace of God he might taste death for everyone.

The quote is from Psalm 8 in which David marveled at God's willingness to give us such a role and prominence. The author of Hebrews quoting this expands the horizon: God's divine purpose was that everything in creation would be subject to man – with no exceptions! Yet the present realities seem to contradict the divine purpose. As we look at our lives, we admit that we do not see everything subject to man. But what we see is Jesus who was made man (a little lower than the angels) who is now crowned with glory and honor! We see one man called Jesus who is crowned with glory and honor – or to put it in Paul's words, we see the man Jesus seated at the right hand of God, far above all rule and authority! This is the very message quoted by Paul in the words of Philippians 2:6-11:

Jesus, being in the very nature of God, did not consider equality with God something to be grasped, but he made himself nothing, taking the very nature of a servant, being made in human likeness.

And being found in the appearance of a man, he humbled himself and became obedient to death – even death on a cross.

Therefore God exalted him to the highest place and gave him a name that is above every name, that at the name of Jesus every knee should bow, in heaven and on earth and under the earth, and every tongue confess that Jesus Christ is Lord, to the glory of God the Father.

In order to restore the purpose of God for man, Jesus became a man and walked in obedience even to death on the cross. He became one of us and was born and died as human. He chose to become family and, in the process, restored our relationship with our heavenly Father by making us his brothers. It cannot be said any more plainly than what we read in Hebrews 2:11-18:

Both the one who makes men holy and those who are made holy are of the same family.
So Jesus is not ashamed to call them brothers.
He says, "I will declare your name to my brothers;
in the presence of the congregation I will sing your praises."

And again, "I will put my trust in him."

And again he says, "Here I am and the children God has given me."

Since the children have flesh and blood, he too shared in their humanity so that by his death he might destroy him who holds the power of death — that is, the devil — and free those who all their lives were held in slavery by their fear of death. For surely, it is not angels he helps, but Abraham's descendants. For this reason. he had to be made like his brothers in every way, in order that he might become a merciful and faithful High Priest in service to God, and that he might make atonement for the sins of the people. Because he himself suffered when he was tempted, he is able to help those who are being tempted.

<u>Let us now return to the very beginning of the chapter and put this all in perspective:</u> The purpose of God is for all of creation to be subject to man. Disobedience allowed Satan and his heavenly host to gain the authority given to man, but in Christ we were chosen even before creation to take our place of authority. He chose to become one of us in obedience to the Father even to death on a cross and paid the price to set us free. Through suffering in obedience, he overcame the enemy and was raised to the supreme authority in the heavens. In him man was reconciled to the Father and is now seated with Christ in the heavenly realms. In him we are empowered to do the very works God ordained for us from before the foundation of the earth – including bringing all of creation into submission as part of the corporate body of Christ. As Paul said, *"God's intent was that through the church, this manifold wisdom of God should be made known to the rulers and authorities in the heavenly realms."* Ephesians 3:10. These rulers and authorities are none other than the devil and his host, *"for our battle is not against flesh and blood, but against the rulers, against the authorities, against the powers of this dark world and against the spiritual forces in the heavenly realms"* See Ephesians 6:12.

We were created for battle and to conquer. God's intent is for us to declare the manifold wisdom of God displayed in the cross to the enemy and to enforce the victory of our Lord. It involves the whole church working in unity and each member has to do the good works for which he/she was created. This is the very heart of the message Paul wrote in Ephesians 4, beginning with the unity and allowing everyone the room to be all that God ordained them to be. Then the clear outline of the fivefold ministry gifts called to prepare all God's people for their divinely appointed ministries:

> _It was Jesus who gave some to be apostles, some to be prophets, some to be evangelists and some to be pastors and teachers, to prepare God's people for works of service, so that the body of Christ may be built up until we all reach unity in the faith and in the knowledge of the Son of God and become mature, attaining to the whole measure of the fullness of Christ._
>
> _Then we will no longer be like infants, tossed back and forth by the waves, and blown here and there by every word of teaching and by the cunning and craftiness of men in their deceitful scheming. Instead, speaking the truth in love, we will in all things grow up in him who is the head, that is, Christ. From him the whole body, joined and held together by every supporting ligament, grows and builds itself up in love, as each part does its work._ Ephesians 4:11-16.

Make no mistake, the church has a task and that is to win the battle. In this it is very important to note that the current model of the Levitical priesthood will not work. A select few "anointed leaders" performing the same old duties will never overcome the enemy! Each part of the body is to be fully released to do its work! The task of the members is not to serve a few select leaders who stand on a platform or behind a pulpit, but it is to subdue the enemy. Listen again to the word of God in Hebrews 10:9-14:

Then he (that is Jesus) said, "Here I am, I have come to do your will." He sets aside the first to establish the second. And by that will, we have been made holy through the sacrifice of the body of Jesus once and for all.

Day after day the (Levitical) priest stands and performs his religious duties; again and again he offers the same sacrifices, which can never take away sins. But when this priest had offered for all time one sacrifice for sins he sat down at the right hand of God. <u>Since that time, he waits for his enemies to be made his footstool, because by one sacrifice he has made perfect forever those who are being made holy.</u>

Our High Priest is waiting. He finished the work and sat at the right hand of the father where he waits for his enemies to be made a footstool. He has given us this task to overcome the enemy. It involves warfare and also what so many in the church fear most – suffering! It is time to face the truth!

PERFECTION THROUGH SUFFERING

We are called and equipped by God to war against the enemy and subdue every enemy to make them a footstool of our Lord. In 2 Corinthians 10:3-5 Paul spoke about this when he wrote:

For though we live in the world, we do not wage war as the world does. The weapons we fight with are not the weapons of the world. On the contrary, they have divine power to demolish strongholds. <u>We demolish arguments and every pretension that sets itself up against the knowledge of God, and we take captive every thought to make it obedient to Christ.</u>

We are called and commissioned to demolish the strongholds of the enemy. These are then defined as mindsets that are opposed to God and pretensions that are set up against the knowledge of God. These are changed as we take thoughts captive and bring these thoughts and thought patterns in obedience to Christ. The goal is to get to that point of obedience that we will walk in the will of God. **The first step in warfare is to deal with our own minds and bring them into line with God's will.** This is what Romans 12:1-2 is all about:

> *Therefore, I urge you, brothers, in view of God's mercy, to offer your bodies as living sacrifices, holy and pleasing to God – this is your spiritual act of worship. <u>Do not conform any longer to the pattern of this world, but be transformed by the renewing of your mind. Then you will be able to test and approve what God's will is – his good, pleasing and perfect will.</u>*

The key to becoming effective warriors is to first tear down our own personal and corporate strongholds. We need to bring our minds in conformity with the eternal will of God. This will is revealed to us as we seek divine wisdom revealed by the Spirit. Let us read how Paul expressed this in 1 Corinthians 2:6-16:

> <u>*We do, however, speak a message of wisdom among the mature, but not the wisdom of this age or of the rulers of this age, who are coming to nothing. No, we speak of God's secret wisdom, a wisdom that has been hidden and that God has destined for our glory before time began.*</u> *None of the rulers of this age understood it, for if they had, they would not have crucified the Lord of glory. However, as it is written,*

> *No eye has seen, no ear has heard, no mind has conceived*

But God has revealed it to us by his Spirit!

The Spirit searches all things, even the deep things of God. For who among men knows the thoughts of a man except the man's spirit within him? In the same way no one knows the thoughts of God, except the Spirit of God. <u>We have not received the spirit of the world, but the Spirit of God, that we may understand what God has freely given us</u>. This is what we speak, not in words of human wisdom, but in words taught by the Spirit, expressing spiritual truths in spiritual words. The man without the Spirit does not accept the things that come from the Spirit of God, for they are foolishness to him, and he cannot understand them, because they are spiritually discerned. The spiritual man makes judgments about all things, but he himself is not subject to any man's judgments:

"For who has known the mind of the Lord that he may instruct him?"

<u>But we have the mind of Christ</u>."

Let us put this together with the words we read in Romans 12. Through the renewal of our minds we bring them into conformity with the mind of Christ. We begin to understand the will and desires of God and his plan for our lives. <u>As we do this not just individually but also corporately, the manifold wisdom of God is revealed to us and through us. As we have seen in the previous chapter, the divine purpose of the church is to make this manifold wisdom known to the rulers and authorities in the heavenly realms in accordance with God's eternal purpose, which he accomplished in Christ (see again Ephesians 3:10-12).</u>

Spiritual warfare is the declaration of God's purposes to the enemy and in doing this we have the authority to bind every spirit of opposition and bring them into submission to Christ. Our authority is rooted in Christ's victory on the cross. However, this authority is exercised by declaring the will of God in the heavenly realms. This is beautifully illustrated in Revelation 12, the sign of the woman and the dragon. As the picture unfolds, we read about the war in heaven between the angelic hosts and how the Dragon, identified as Satan, and his angels lost their place in heaven and were hurled down to earth (Revelation 12:7-9). Then we read the following:

Then I heard a loud voice in heaven say:

"Now have come the salvation and the power and the kingdom of our God, and <u>the authority of his Christ</u>. For the accuser of our brothers, who accuses them before our God day and night has been hurled down.

<u>*They overcame him by the blood of the lamb and by the word of their testimony. They did not love their lives so much as to shrink from death.*</u> *Therefore rejoice, you heavens, and you who dwell in them!*

<u>*But woe to the earth and the sea, because the devil has gone down to you! He is filled with fury, because he knows his time is short."*</u> Revelation 12:10-12.

As we read this it is very important to note the very things we often fail to quote from these well-known verses: They overcame by the blood of the lamb and the word of their testimony – and <u>they were willing to die because of this testimony!</u>

In the Western world and particularly here in North America, we have a tremendous fear of suffering. Thus, we have developed a theology that denies suffering. The Word Faith Movement with the truth that it presents has taken that to the extreme and many now claim that as Jesus paid the price, we do not have to suffer today. In addition, we have developed the concept of the rapture – a term that is not found in Scripture at all. The idea being that when things get tough, we will be spared the suffering. Now, this is not the time and place to discuss these doctrines, but <u>let us look at what God says about suffering in the church.</u>

First, no one who claims to be a believer will disagree that Jesus is our model for a victorious life on earth. He lived the perfect life and never sinned. That is why he was declared to be the High Priest in the order of Melchizedek. Now, let us read Hebrews 5:5-10:

> *During the days of Jesus' life on earth, he offered up prayers and petitions with loud cries and tears to the one who could save him from death, and <u>he was heard because of his reverent submission. Although he was a son, he learned obedience from what he suffered and, once made perfect, he became the source of eternal salvation for all those who obey him, and he was designated by God to be High Priest in the order of Melchizedek.</u>*

Let us note that Jesus learned obedience by his suffering! Let us also note that his prayers were heard because of his reverent submission. This is nowhere more clearly illustrated than in the garden of Gethsemane. We read that Jesus wrestled in prayer to the point of sweating blood, but ultimately settled the issue by submission to the will of God. In the words of Philippians 2:8 *"being found in appearance as a man he humbled himself and became obedient to death - even death on a cross!"*

Contrary to the teaching of many in our western churches, Jesus expected that those who follow him would endure persecution. He stated that many times, e.g. John 15:18-21:

> *If the world hates you, keep in mind that it hated me first. If you belonged to the world, it would love you as its own. As it is, you do not belong to the world, but I have chosen you out of the world. That is why the world hates you. Remember the words I spoke to you: "No servant is greater than his master." If they persecuted me, they will persecute you also. If they obeyed my teaching, they will obey yours also. They will treat you this way because of my name, for they do not know the One who sent me.*

Also, when talking to the disciples about the coming age, he stated this in no uncertain terms when he spoke the words recorded in Luke 21:12-19:

> *But before all this, they will lay hands on you and persecute you. They will deliver you to synagogues and prisons, and you will be brought before kings and governors, and all on account of my name. This will result in your being witnesses to them.*

But make up your mind not to worry beforehand how you will defend yourselves. For I will give you words and wisdom that none of your adversaries will be able to resist or contradict. You will be betrayed even by parents, brothers, relatives and friends, and they will put some of you to death. All men will hate you because of me. But not a hair of your head will perish. By standing firm you will gain life.

In the light of this expectation, Jesus spoke forth a blessing on those who are being persecuted and he also warned the disciples not to retaliate, but to bless those who persecute them. We find this in the Sermon on the Mount, Matthew 5:11-12 and 43-48:

Blessed are you when people insult you, persecute you and falsely say all kinds of evil against you because of me. Rejoice and be glad, because great is your reward in heaven, for in the same way they persecuted the prophets who were before you.

You have heard that it was said, "Love your neighbor and hate your enemy." But I tell you: Love your enemies and pray for those who persecute you, that you may be sons of your Father in heaven. He causes his sun to rise on the evil and the good, and sends rain on the righteous and the unrighteous. If you love those who love you, what reward will you get? Are not even the tax collectors doing that? And if you greet only your brothers, what are you doing more than others? Do not even pagans do that? Be perfect, therefore, as your heavenly Father is perfect.

As we follow the story of the church, we know it actually happened very soon after the birth of the church on the day of Pentecost. In Acts 7 and 8 we read of the martyrdom of Stephen and how that triggered a major persecution of the believers. Saul led this persecution, until the Lord stopped him on his way to Damascus. With his conversion the persecution ended for a season, but Paul himself experienced severe persecution at times as he planted churches and shared the message of Christ, e. g. in Psidian Antioch (see Acts 13:49-50) and later in Philippi where he and Silas were beaten and imprisoned (see Acts 16). In fact, Paul spoke about some of the sufferings he endured in 2 Corinthians 11:23-29:

> *I am more. I have worked much harder, been in prison more frequently, been flogged more severely, and been exposed to death again and again. Five times I received from the Jews the forty lashes minus one. Three times I was beaten with rods, once I was stoned, three times I was shipwrecked, I spent a night and a day in the open sea, I have been constantly on the move. I have been in danger from rivers, in danger from bandits, in danger from my own countrymen, in danger from Gentiles; in danger in the city, in danger in the country, in danger at sea; and in danger from false brothers. I have labored and toiled and have often gone without sleep; I have known hunger and thirst and have often gone without food; I have been cold and naked. Besides everything else, I face daily the pressure of my concern for all the churches. Who is weak, and I do not feel weak? Who is led into sin, and I do not inwardly burn?*

Why did Paul suffer all of these things? Let us listen to his words spoken to King Agrippa as recorded in Acts 26:15-23 where he related the story of what happened to him on the road to Damascus many years earlier:

Then I asked, "Who are you Lord?"

"I am Jesus, whom you are persecuting," the Lord replied. "Now get up and stand on your feet. I have appeared to you to appoint you as a servant and as a witness of what you have seen of me and what I will show you. I will rescue you from your own people and from the Gentiles. I am sending you to them to open their eyes and turn them from darkness to light, and from the power of Satan to God, so that they may receive forgiveness of sins and a place among those who are sanctified by faith in me."

<u>So then, King Agrippa, I was not disobedient to the vision from heaven.</u> First to those in Damascus, then to those in Jerusalem and in all Judea, and to the Gentiles also, I preached that they should repent and turn to God and prove their repentance by their deeds. That is why the Jews seized me in the temple courts and tried to kill me. But I have had God's help to this very day, and so I stand here and testify to small and great alike. I am saying nothing beyond what the prophets and Moses said would happen - that the Christ would suffer and, as the first to rise from the dead, would proclaim light to his own people and to the Gentiles.

When Paul met the risen Lord, our High Priest in the order of Melchizedek, his life was radically changed. <u>The vision he received became the guiding light for his life and he was willing to be obedient whatever the cost. In his own words in Philippians 3:7-21:</u>

But whatever was to my profit I now consider loss for the sake of Christ. What is more, I consider everything a loss compared to the surpassing greatness of knowing Christ Jesus my Lord, for whose sake I have lost all things. I consider them rubbish, *that I may gain Christ and be found in him, not having a righteousness of my own that comes from the law, but that which is through faith in Christ-the righteousness that comes from God and is by faith. <u>I want to know Christ and the power of his resurrection and the fellowship of sharing in his sufferings, becoming like him in his death, and so, somehow, to attain to the resurrection from the dead.</u>*

<u>Not that I have already obtained all this, or have already been made perfect, but I press on to take hold of that for which Christ Jesus took hold of me.</u> Brothers, I do not consider myself yet to have taken hold of it. But one thing I do: Forgetting what is behind and straining toward what is ahead, I press on toward the goal to win the prize for which God has called me heavenward in Christ Jesus.

<u>All of us who are mature should take such a view of things.</u> And if on some point you think differently, that too God will make clear to you. Only let us live up to what we have already attained.

<u>Join with others in following my example, brothers, and take note of those who live according to the pattern we gave you.</u> For, as I have often told you before and now say again even with tears, many live as enemies of the cross of Christ. Their destiny is destruction, their god is their stomach, and their glory is in their shame. Their mind is on earthly things. But our citizenship is in heaven. And we eagerly await a Savior from there, the Lord Jesus Christ, who, by the power that enables him to bring everything under his control, will transform our lowly bodies so that they will be like his glorious body.

Let us get the picture in proper perspective: Paul met the risen Jesus, declared to be High Priest in the order of Melchizedek, and his life was totally changed. In the dust on the road to Damascus he had a vision for which he was willing to give everything he had and he stayed true to that vision. That vision included the suffering he was to experience as revealed to Ananias by the Lord (Acts 9:15-16):

But the Lord said to Ananias, "Go! This man is my chosen instrument to carry my name before the Gentiles and their kings and before the people of Israel. I will show him how much he must suffer for my name."

Paul understood that as Christians we are not exempt from suffering. He was not just an example of this fact, but he also taught that to the believers and they experienced persecution and suffering just as he did, e.g. Philippians 1:27-30:

Whatever happens, conduct yourselves in a manner worthy of the gospel of Christ. Then, whether I come and see you or only hear about you in my absence, I will know that you stand firm in one spirit, contending as one man for the faith of the gospel without being frightened in any way by those who oppose you. This is a sign to them that they will be destroyed, but that you will be saved - and that by God. <u>For it has been granted to you on behalf of Christ not only to believe on him, but also to suffer for him, since you are going through the same struggle you saw I had, and now hear that I still have.</u>

Likewise, the church in Thessalonica was birthed amidst persecution (Acts 17:1-10) and Paul wrote to them in 1 Thessalonians 1:4-8:

> *For we know, brothers loved by God, that he has chosen you, because our gospel came to you not simply with words, but also with power, with the Holy Spirit and with deep conviction. You know how we lived among you for your sake. <u>You became imitators of us and of the Lord; in spite of severe suffering, you welcomed the message with the joy given by the Holy Spirit.</u> And so you became a model to all the believers in Macedonia and Achaia. The Lord's message rang out from you not only in Macedonia and Achaia - your faith in God has become known everywhere.*

As leader Paul was not alone in this. Peter also wrote about this in 1 Peter 4:1-2 and 12-19:

> *Therefore, since Christ suffered in his body, arm yourselves also with the same attitude, because he who has suffered in his body is done with sin. As a result, he does not live the rest of his earthly life for evil human desires, but rather for the will of God.*

> *Dear friends, do not be surprised at the painful trial you are suffering, as though something strange were happening to you. But rejoice that you participate in the sufferings of Christ, so that you may be overjoyed when his glory is revealed. If you are insulted because of the name of Christ, you are blessed, for the Spirit of glory and of God rests on you. If you suffer, it should not be as a murderer or thief or any other kind of criminal or even a meddler. However, if you suffer as a Christian do not be ashamed, but praise God that you bear that name. For it is time for judgment to begin with the family of God; and if it*

> *begins with us, what will the outcome be for those who do not obey the gospel of God? And, "If it is hard for the righteous to be saved, what will become of the ungodly and the sinner?"*
>
> *So then, those who suffer according to God's will should commit themselves to their faithful Creator and continue to do good.*

Likewise, James wrote about it in James 1:2-4 and many of the apostolic leaders suffered greatly. Our High Priest learned obedience through his suffering and became perfected. Suffering is a divine tool to bring us to perfection and submission to the will of God. The very power of God is released in our weakness. We first learn to use the powerful divine weapons designed to pull down strongholds by taking our own thoughts captive and bring them to obedience in Christ and we need to do this until we have the mind of Christ. This is why our bodies must be placed on the altar as living sacrifices until our minds are no longer conformed to the world and we are able to do the will of God – <u>even if it calls for severe suffering. In this way we become the holy priesthood in the order of Melchizedek and we are able to offer spiritual sacrifices acceptable to God.</u> 1 Peter 2:4-9 and Romans 12:1 -2:

The North American mindset towards suffering is nothing less than a stronghold that has to be demolished. If we could overcome simply by "binding" the enemy and "loosing" the suffering as some would have us believe, Paul and the other early apostles could have been saved from much suffering. A great deal of the "spiritual warfare" in the church is nothing else than self-deception and comes from immaturity. Many of us are children and spiritual teenagers. Much of the church in the West is like the Hebrews and the admonition in Hebrews 12:1-12 is one we should heed:

> *Therefore, since we are surrounded by such a great cloud of witnesses, let us throw off everything that hinders and the sin that so easily entangles, and let us run with perseverance the race marked out for us. Let us fix our eyes on Jesus, the author and perfecter of our faith, who for the joy set before him endured the cross, scorning its shame, and sat down at the right hand of the throne of God. Consider him who endured such opposition from sinful men, so that you will not grow weary and lose heart.*

> *In your struggle against sin, you have not yet resisted to the point of shedding your blood. And you have forgotten that word of encouragement that addresses you as sons:*

> *"My son, do not make light of the Lord's discipline,*
> *and do not lose heart when he rebukes you,*
> *because the Lord disciplines those he loves,*
> *and he punishes everyone he accepts as a son."*

> *Endure hardship as discipline; God is treating you as sons. For what son is not disciplined by his father? If you are not disciplined (and everyone undergoes discipline), then you are illegitimate children and not true sons. Moreover, we have all had human fathers who disciplined us and we respected them for it. How much more should we submit to the Father of our spirits and live! Our fathers disciplined us for a little while as they thought best; but God disciplines us for our good, that we may share in his holiness. No discipline seems pleasant at*

*the time, but painful. Later on, however, it produces a harvest
of righteousness and peace for those who have been trained by
it. Therefore, strengthen your feeble arms and weak knees.
"Make level paths for your feet," so that the lame may not
be disabled, but rather healed. Make every effort to live in
peace with all men and to be holy; without holiness no one
will see the Lord.*

In fact, in an earlier passage the author reminded the
Hebrews of the earlier days and how their faith led them
to stand their ground in the contest, Hebrews 10:32-36:

*Remember those earlier days after you had received the light, when
you stood your ground in a great contest in the face of suffering.
Sometimes you were publicly exposed to insult and persecution; at
other times you stood side by side with those who were so treated.
You sympathized with those in prison and joyfully accepted the
confiscation of your property, because you knew that you yourselves
had better and lasting possessions. So do not throw away your
confidence; it will be richly rewarded. You need to persevere so
that when you have done the will of God, you will receive what
he has promised.*

Note the last words quoted: We are to persevere so that
when we have done the will of God, we will receive what
he has promised. Another way of saying this is that we
need to overcome in order to claim the inheritance we
have in Christ. In him we have received the Spirit and
we have an obligation to overcome the flesh and live in
the freedom given in Christ. This is the heart of Paul's
message in Romans 8. Let us read Romans 8:14-17 and

see how suffering is the way to glory and the very thing
that reveals the sons of God:

> *Those who are led by the Spirit of God are sons of God. For
> you did not receive a spirit that makes you a slave again to
> fear, but you received the Spirit of sonship. And by him we
> cry, "Abba, Father." The Spirit himself testifies with our
> spirit that we are God's children. <u>Now if we are children,
> then we are heirs - heirs of God and co-heirs with Christ, if
> indeed we share in his sufferings in order that we may also
> share in his glory.</u>*

In Hebrews 12:2 we read that *Jesus for the joy set before him
endured the cross, scorning its shame, and sat down at the right
hand of the throne of God.* As we keep our eyes fixed on him
who is the author and finisher of our faith (Hebrews
12:1-2), we will likewise find that our suffering does not
compare to the future inheritance. In Paul's words in
Romans 8:18:

> *I consider that our present sufferings are not worth comparing
> with the glory that will be revealed in us.*

It is in this context that Paul later says in Rom 8:28-30:

> *And we know that in all things God works for the good of
> those who love him, who have been called according to his
> purpose. For those God foreknew he also predestined to be
> conformed to the likeness of his Son, that he might be the
> firstborn among many brothers. And those he predestined, he
> also called; those he called, he also justified; those he justified,
> he also glorified.*

There is a lot more we will look at later, particularly the aspect of God's glory released in us. However, before we move there, we need to consider a very important aspect of Jesus' suffering which took place outside the walls of the city.

OUTSIDE THE GATE

The high priest carries the blood of animals into the Most Holy Place as a sin offering, but the bodies are burned outside the camp. And so Jesus also suffered outside the city gate to make the people holy through his own blood. Let us, then, go to him outside the camp, bearing the disgrace he bore. For here we do not have an enduring city, but we are looking for the city that is to come. Hebrews 13:11-12.

As we have studied the order of Melchizedek, we have seen that Jesus is the eternal High Priest. His death took place on a hill outside the city of Jerusalem where he died on the cross. In a very real way, he became a sacrifice for our sins. As the body of the animal sacrificed for remission of sins was burnt outside the camp, so Jesus died outside of the city gate. As he died, he paid the price and became the cornerstone of a spiritual temple, which is built through us as living stones into a holy nation, a kingdom of priests (see 1 Peter 2:4-10). In the words of Isaiah 53:3-6:

He was despised and rejected by men,
a man of sorrows, and familiar with suffering.
Like one from whom men hide their faces
he was despised, and we esteemed him not.
Surely, he took up our infirmities
and carried our sorrows,
yet we considered him stricken by God,
smitten by him, and afflicted.

But he was pierced for our transgressions,
he was crushed for our iniquities;
the punishment that brought us peace was upon him,
and by his wounds we are healed.
We all, like sheep, have gone astray,
each of us has turned to his own way;
and the LORD has laid on him the iniquity of us all.

Through his suffering we became holy and included into his family. As he was willing to be numbered with us as transgressors, <u>we are encouraged to go outside the camp, bearing the disgrace he bore.</u> As we seek to understand this admonition, we need to look at a very important festival in Israel called the Feast of Tabernacles. This was the third major pilgrimage feast in Israel, the other two being Passover and Pentecost. These were known as pilgrimage festivals, because during these festivals the Israelites traveled to Jerusalem for the celebrations. Each festival was of agricultural significance and at the same time commemorating significant historical events in the life of the nation. The first of these is Passover, which is connected with the barley harvest. At the same time, it also recalls the exodus from Egypt (Ex. 12:6; Lev. 23:5,8; Num. 28:16-25 and Deut. 16:1-8). Pentecost is the celebration of the wheat harvest and when the first fruits are brought to the sanctuary; it also recalls the day of the giving of the Law (Ex 34:26; Lev 23:10-14; Num 28:26-31). The Feast of Tabernacles celebrates the gathering of the harvest; it recalls the beginnings of the wanderings in the wilderness (Ex. 23:16; Lev. 23:33 ff; Deut. 16:13-15).

We do not want to get side tracked, but it is important to make some observations. Each of these feasts is a shadow of the work and ministry of Jesus. Passover is a type of the redemption that came through Jesus. As Israel was set free from bondage in Egypt, Passover and the feast of unleavened bread speak of the freedom from sin that came through Jesus. He is our Passover lamb who died and whose blood has set us free. The feast of Pentecost signals the beginning of the harvest. It became the day that Jesus' promise was fulfilled as the Holy Spirit was poured out and the church was birthed. The believers became the first fruits of the harvest and a symbol of the coming ingathering. The feast of Tabernacles portrays the end time harvest and the consummation of the work of Christ in and through the church.

Most of the above is not new to the church. These three feasts also correlate to the three-part division of the tabernacle. The outer court had the altar and the basins for water symbolizing the death of Christ and the purification through his blood and baptism – similar to the redemption celebrated in Passover. The Holy place contained the altar for incense, the golden lamp stand and the tables with showbread. These symbolized the presence and provision of God through his Spirit and correspond to Pentecost. The Most Holy Place that was separated from the rest of the sanctuary, housed the Ark of the Covenant with the mercy seat. It was the place of the very presence of God filled with his glory. This corresponds to the feast of Tabernacles when God will tabernacle with his people and his glory will fill the earth.

Now let us return to the passage we read in Hebrews 13 where we were encouraged to move outside the walls through the gate and bear the disgrace that Jesus bore. With that in mind, let us <u>read Leviticus 23:39-43:</u>

> *So beginning with the fifteenth day of the seventh month, after you have gathered the crops of the land, celebrate the festival to the LORD for seven days; the first day is a day of rest, and the eighth day also is a day of rest. On the first day you are to take choice fruit from the trees, and palm fronds, leafy branches and poplars, and rejoice before the LORD your God for seven days. Celebrate this as a festival to the LORD for seven days each year. This is to be a lasting ordinance for the generations to come; celebrate it in the seventh month. <u>Live in booths for seven days: All native-born Israelites are to live in booths so your descendants will know that I had the Israelites live in booths when I brought them out of Egypt. I am the LORD your God.</u>*

It is very important to look at the fact that they were to live in booths, which were temporary shelters constructed with branches and leaves. To live in booths meant that they had to move outside of the regular comfort zone of their homes into the fields. As we also see it is tied to the ingathering of the harvest. The feast of Tabernacles is the fulfillment of the promise of Pentecost, because Pentecost represented the first fruits as promise of the coming harvest. <u>I believe the coming harvest will only be gathered in, as the church moves out of the current structure based on the Levitical priesthood.</u> In the words of Hebrews 13 quoted above, we are to move outside the camp. The church was never meant to be locked into the Levitical order with its priests (called pastors) and the supporting cast of Levites ministering to the "laity" within the safety and security of the four walls of a man-made sanctuary. We were called and commissioned to move outside of the camp and into the world. This cannot be said any more clearly than Jesus' parting words recorded in Matthew 28:18-19:

> *Then Jesus came to them and said, "All authority in heaven and on earth has been given to me. Therefore, go and make disciples of all nations, baptizing them in the name of the Father and of the Son and of the Holy Spirit, and teaching them to obey everything I have commanded you. And surely, I am with you always, to the very end of the age."*

Let us look at this from another angle. In Hebrews 9 the author describes the worship in the earthly tabernacle under the Levitical order. Then in Hebrews 9:6-10 he continues:

When everything had been arranged like this, the priests entered regularly into the outer room to carry on their ministry. But only the high priest entered the inner room, and that only once a year, and never without blood, which he offered for himself and for the sins the people had committed in ignorance. <u>The Holy Spirit was showing by this that the way into the Most Holy Place had not yet been disclosed as long as the first tabernacle was still standing.</u> This is an illustration for the present time, indicating that the gifts and sacrifices being offered were not able to clear the conscience of the worshiper. They are only a matter of food and drink and various ceremonial washings - external regulations applying until the time of the new order.

As we have seen in the previous chapters, the church, as we know it is based on a semi-Christianized version of the Levitical order. With the conversion of Emperor Constantine in Rome there was a radical departure from the apostolic model birthed at Pentecost. This effectively meant that the way into the Most Holy Place was again being veiled and it literally led to what we call "the Dark Ages." The Reformation and the subsequent changes in the church have not affected its structure. As a result, the promise of Pentecost has not led to the feast of Tabernacles with the end-time harvest. The cyclical rituals repeated endlessly in the church buildings have not touched the world. The modern priests and Levites managing and overseeing the programs to cater to the spiritual needs of the believers are not effectively changing our communities and reaching the lost. <u>As long as our Levitical order with its earthly tabernacles are still in standing, the way into the Most Holy Place</u>

will remain a mystery to most in the church, for they will continue to stay in their comfort zones where the clergy and their Levites will be the paid professionals ministering to the saved.

There is a sense of safety and comfort within the camp and within the walls. Outside we live in temporary shelters in small family units. Outside in the wilderness we bear the disgrace that our High Priest bore. To use the picture of Hebrews 13:12 we have to move outside of the gate. This is a very interesting term. The gate represents the place of control into and out of the city. The gatekeeper could open and close the gate to keep people in or out. It is interesting to note that there is a growing tendency for pastors to see themselves as "the spiritual gatekeepers" in our city and community. The gate is also the place of where legal matters were settled. In a symbolic way Jesus had to go through the gate (judgment by the Levitical order) to suffer and die outside. Those who choose to leave the comfort of our local Levitical structures will have to go through the gate into the wilderness. In the process they will need to pass by the gatekeepers who have a vested interest in controlling the gate to maintain the structure and their positions. Like Jesus, those who pass through the gate, will face judgment and rejection and have to bear the disgrace he bore.

To leave through the gate has a huge price tag. It is tied to rejection and suffering. We saw that in the previous chapter. It is the choice between the fear of God and the fear of man and those who do not shrink back will be rewarded. It only comes when we step out in faith and in obedience. This is the heart of the message penned down in Hebrews 11 where we find example after example of people who risked everything for the heavenly vision and were willing to suffer and die because of their faith. Following this powerful picture of the heroes of faith, we read in Hebrews 12:1-3:

> *Therefore, since we are surrounded by such a great cloud of witnesses, let us throw off everything that hinders and the sin that so easily entangles, and let us run with perseverance the race marked out for us. Let us fix our eyes on Jesus, the author and perfecter of our faith, who for the joy set before him endured the cross, scorning its shame, and sat down at the right hand of the throne of God. Consider him who endured such opposition from sinful men, so that you will not grow weary and lose heart.*

God is seeking people of faith who can see beyond the first fruits of Pentecost and recognize that the fields are ready for the harvest. Jesus is calling a people who will follow him in obedience and will allow him to perfect the faith he birthed in them, even at the cost of suffering and death. Our Lord is searching for those who will throw off everything that hinders them in order that they may run the race marked out for them with perseverance. He is calling forth those who have the courage to walk through the gate of misunderstanding, religious control and judgment into the wilderness to live in temporary shelters in order that they may gather the harvest.

Those who are willing to venture outside and be the church in the world will gather this end time harvest. In the booths erected in the fields there was not room for many and they housed mostly family units. The booths represent the local homes and businesses where individuals and families open their lives to God and invite him to tabernacle with them. The presence and power of God was never intended only for a few with worldly certificates and credentials and titles. This was already clear on the day of Pentecost when the Holy Spirit fell on all – men and women, old and young, learned and unlearned. In Christ as head, the whole body is included in the order of Melchizedek and everyone is anointed as holy priest and appointed to ministry. Jesus Christ opened the way for every individual to enter into the presence of God and to experience the glory. Every one of us can tabernacle with God and be in his glorious presence. Those that understand this message know the Spirit and walk in freedom. They do not need the permission of a man to be obedient to their call and mission. They do not have to seek to be released by "the pastor" to do their work and they know that they need no covering from any human. They are covered by the Lord just as Israel was covered during the wanderings in the desert. They hear his voice and know they have authority in his name to drive out demons, lay hands on the sick and set the captives free. As we move beyond Pentecost to the feast of Tabernacles, individuals and family units with local homes will be the crucial units for the harvest. The old Levitical order with its buildings and priestly hierarchies will give way to home churches. In the local homes and businesses, lives will be changed as ordinary people do the works of Jesus and even greater works as he himself said in John 14:12. The home churches and other small churches e.g. in schools and businesses will be full churches supporting one another as directed by the Spirit. As they link together in a network they will be served by apostles, prophets, evangelists, pastors and teachers who will be itinerant workers equipping the saints. They will serve and lead through relationship and not control. This network will become the net to draw the catch for the end time harvest.

However, the first step is to walk through the gate into the wilderness. This is a very difficult step for most, especially for those currently serving in the Levitical order. I know this from personal experience for when you walk through the gate, you are judged and many doors close. To choose to leave the comfort of home and tabernacle in the wilderness in a makeshift temporary structure is very scary – especially if you are a Levite and you leave the security offered by the priestly benefits and depend entirely on God to meet your needs. To lay aside your Levitical traditions and attitudes are not easy – particularly to deal with those who are "less qualified" than you, but who walk in a stronger anointing! Likewise, it is very difficult for those who have walked out but have been severely wounded by the Levitical system. Some have been treated as second-class citizens for so long, they cannot really accept that in the order of Melchizedek they are true sons and daughters, anointed and appointed to serve the King of Kings. Some struggle with the freedom, as they have never been allowed to be free! Whatever the case may be – we have to move through the gate and into the wilderness to move beyond Pentecost. Let us follow the example of our Lord and go through the gate!

INTO THE WILDERNESS

As we have seen in the previous chapter, the church has to move through the gate as Jesus did. The experiences of Passover where we celebrate our freedom through the blood of the Lamb and Pentecost where we rejoice in the baptism of the Spirit are great and glorious. But there is more and the next feast in our pilgrimage is the feast of Tabernacles, which calls us out of the security of our comfort zones through the gate into the wilderness to live in temporary dwellings.

To understand this journey into the wilderness we need to go back to the history of Israel. They celebrated Passover and rejoiced as they were set free from the bondage in Egypt and saved in a miraculous way when God led them through the Red Sea. From there they traveled to Sinai where they received the law to guide them as the people of God. The giving of the law was celebrated at the time of Pentecost. They continued to travel and camp in the wilderness for about two years. Then they traveled to the edge of the Promised Land and the twelve spies were sent into the land. They returned and the majority report of ten spies caused the people to rebel and refuse to enter the land. Because of the disobedience and rebellion, God forced them to stay in the wilderness for another 38 years and that generation died in the wilderness. During the ingathering of the harvest the Israelites celebrated the feast of Tabernacles. As we have seen during this feast they lived in booths. These reminded them of the forty years in the wilderness where the older disobedient generation died and a new generation prepared to enter the Promised Land.

<u>In this context the feast of Tabernacles is a shadow of the church being prepared to enter the fullness of God's promise.</u> Let us turn again to the letter to the Hebrews and look at the third chapter, which compares the church to the tabernacle. Moses as faithful servant built the tabernacle. However, Jesus is greater than Moses and he is faithful as son over God's new house, the church (see Hebrews 3:1-6). Then we read: Hebrews 3:6-11:

> *<u>But Christ is faithful as a son over God's house. And we are his house, if we hold on to our courage and the hope of which we boast.</u>*

> *So, as the Holy Spirit says:*

"Today, if you hear his voice, do not harden your hearts as you did in the rebellion,

during the time of testing in the desert, where your fathers tested and tried me

and for forty years saw what I did.

That is why I was angry with that generation, and I said,

`Their hearts are always going astray, and they have not known my ways.'

<u>*So I declared on oath in my anger, 'They shall never enter my rest.'"*</u>

In this there is a very serious warning to the church. Israel missed the appointed time to enter the land as they rebelled. In the process they failed to enter into the Sabbath rest for God's people. To understand this, we need to read further (Hebrews 3:16-4:11):

Who were they who heard and rebelled? Were they not all those Moses led out of Egypt? And with whom was he angry for forty years? Was it not with those who sinned, whose bodies fell in the desert? And to whom did God swear that they would never enter his rest if not to those who disobeyed? So, we see that they were not able to enter, because of their unbelief.

<u>*Therefore, since the promise of entering his rest still stands, let us be careful that none of you be found to have fallen short of it. For we also have had the gospel preached to us, just as they did; but the message they heard was of no value to them, because those who heard did not combine it with faith. Now*</u>

*we who have believed enter that rest, just as God has said,
"So I declared on oath in my anger, `They shall never enter
my rest.'"*

*And yet his work has been finished since the creation of the
world. For somewhere he has spoken about the seventh day in
these words: "And on the seventh day God rested from all his
work." And again, in the passage above he says, "They shall
never enter my rest." <u>It still remains that some will enter that
rest, and those who formerly had the gospel preached to them
did not go in, because of their disobedience. Therefore, God
again set a certain day, calling it Today, when a long time
later he spoke through David, as was said before: "Today, if
you hear his voice, do not harden your hearts."</u> For if Joshua
had given them rest, God would not have spoken later about
another day. <u>There remains, then, a Sabbath-rest for the
people of God; for anyone who enters God's rest also rests from
his own work, just as God did from his. Let us, therefore,
make every effort to enter that rest, so that no one will fall by
following their example of disobedience.</u>*

When we consider that it is written in 2 Peter 3:8, *"With
the Lord a day is like a thousand years, and a thousand years are
like a day,"* an interesting picture presents itself. In terms
of the Biblical timeline we are moving into the seventh
day from Adam. This means we have the opportunity
to enter into the Sabbath rest. Moreover, in terms of
Jesus Christ, we are entering into the Third Day. This
is very important as we consider that Jesus rose from
the grave early in the morning on the third day after
he died. More importantly, though, we need to listen
to the prophetic words regarding the church and the
third day. Let us begin with the story in John 2 where

Jesus cleansed the temple. Following that we read in John 2:17-22:

> *His disciples remembered that it is written: "Zeal for your house will consume me."*
>
> *Then the Jews demanded of him, "What miraculous sign can you show us to prove your authority to do all this?"*
>
> *Jesus answered them, "Destroy this temple, and I will raise it again in three days."*
>
> *The Jews replied, "It has taken forty-six years to build this temple, and you are going to raise it in three days?" But the temple he had spoken of was his body. After he was raised from the dead, his disciples recalled what he had said. Then they believed the Scripture and the words that Jesus had spoken.*

Before we continue with this, note that the context of the passage has to do with the zeal for God's house. It is prophetically important to understand that the new house of God of which he is the cornerstone is also described as his body. With that let us move to another very interesting passage in Luke's gospel. Following the execution of John the Baptist Jesus was warned to leave the place, as Herod wanted to kill him too. He then answered in these words (Luke 13:32 NKJV):

> *He replied, "Go tell that fox, `I will drive out demons and heal people today and tomorrow, and on the third day I will be perfected.'"*

Earlier we have read that Jesus became perfect through his sufferings (Hebrews 5:7-10). His body, which is the church, will be perfected on the third day as he intends to build up this temple in three days. For this reason, he gave the five-fold ministry gifts as we read in Ephesians 4:11-16:

> *It was he who gave some to be apostles, some to be prophets, some to be evangelists, and some to be pastors and teachers, to prepare God's people for works of service, so that the body of Christ may be built up until we all reach unity in the faith and in the knowledge of the Son of God and become mature, attaining to the whole measure of the fullness of Christ.*

> *Then we will no longer be infants, tossed back and forth by the waves, and blown here and there by every wind of teaching and by the cunning and craftiness of men in their deceitful scheming. Instead, speaking the truth in love, we will in all things grow up into him who is the Head, that is, Christ. From him the whole body, joined and held together by every supporting ligament, grows and builds itself up in love, as each part does its work.*

In the original Greek the words here translated as "to prepare God's people" and that the body needs to become "mature" is the very same earlier translated as being perfected.

When we put these all together, it implies that the body of Christ, the church, will be perfected on the third day. To enter into the Sabbath rest prepared for God's people, we need to be perfected as his body on earth. Until we are perfected as church, we will not enter the heavenly kingdom. To use another Biblical picture, Jesus will return for a spotless bride without stain or wrinkle. Thus, we are to move out of the security of our man-made structures through the gate and into the place where we will be built up and become perfected as body of Christ. As we move through the gate, we enter the wilderness where we live in temporary shelters and where we learn to tabernacle with God as individuals and families, as Israel did during the journey to the Promised Land.

The wilderness journey is the time of preparation for the church. It is the time of stepping out in faith into the place where there is no security except in and through God himself. It is in that place where we learn to trust in him and his provision. It is the place where we find the truth that we do not need the mediation of an earthly priest, but that each one can tabernacle with God and experience the full access into the Most Holy Place through the veil, that is the body of Christ.

The wilderness is also the place of testing through suffering and temptation. It is precisely to this place that we are led by the Spirit. In a very real way that is what happened with Jesus after his baptism, when the Spirit came upon him. Directly after that the Spirit led him into the desert where he was tempted. It was in the desert that God prepared the Joshua generation. It was also in the desert experience of the Assyrian exile that God spoke the prophetic word to his rebellious nation recorded in Hosea 2:14-20:

"Therefore, I am now going to allure her;

I will lead her into the desert and speak tenderly to her.

There I will give her back her vineyards,

and will make the Valley of Achor a door of hope.

There she will sing as in the days of her youth,

as in the day she came up out of Egypt.

"In that day," declares the LORD, "you will call me `my husband';

you will no longer call me `my master.'

I will remove the names of the Baals from her lips; no longer will their names be invoked.

In that day I will make a covenant for them with the beasts of the field

and the birds of the air and the creatures that move along the ground.

Bow and sword and battle I will abolish from the land, so that all may lie down in safety.

I will betroth you to me forever; I will betroth you in righteousness and justice,

in love and compassion.

> *I will betroth you in faithfulness, and you will acknowledge*
> *the LORD.*

Today the Lord is calling a rebellious church lost in its worldly structures and illegitimate order of priesthood out through the gate to the place of restoration. God is seeking a remnant, willing to go into the wilderness and willing to leave the man-made religious structures in order to experience his presence and glory, even if it means persecution and rejection. The prophetic call of Hosea 6:1-3 is very much the call for the Western church of our day:

> *"Come, let us return to the LORD.*
> *He has torn us to pieces but he will heal us;*
> *he has injured us but he will bind up our wounds.*
> *After two days he will revive us;*
> *on the third day he will restore us,*
> *that we may live in his presence.*
> *Let us acknowledge the LORD;*
> *let us press on to acknowledge him.*
> *As surely as the sun rises, he will appear;*

Let us look at this in more depth. In this third day the Lord is restoring his church. He has invited us to move through the gate out of the four walls and the institutional bureaucracy of the church into the wilderness. He is taking those who respond to his call into the desert to restore the foundations. As we move into the wilderness, we will find that as surely as the sun rises, he will appear. Once again it is illuminating to look at the history of Israel. It was in the desert that they arrived at Sinai and with the exception of Moses no one else had really met the Lord. Here they met the Lord and received the law. They received the blueprint as the people of God for life, both personal and corporate. This event was celebrated in Israel during the feast of Pentecost and in the agricultural environment it signified the first fruits of the harvest, a sign of the great ingathering.

Like Israel, as we move out of bondage (Egypt) into the desert on the way to the Promised Land, we have to stop at Sinai for our Pentecost. This is where God appears to us in a new and powerful way. In the words of Hebrews 12:18-24:

> *You have not come to a mountain that can be touched and that is burning with fire; to darkness, gloom and storm; to a trumpet blast or to such a voice speaking words that those who heard it begged that no further word be spoken to them, because they could not bear what was commanded: "If even an animal touches the mountain, it must be stoned." The sight was so terrifying that Moses said, "I am trembling with fear."*

> *But you have come to Mount Zion, to the heavenly Jerusalem, the city of the living God. You have come to thousands upon thousands of angels in joyful assembly, to the church of the firstborn, whose names are written in heaven. You have come to God, the judge of all men, to the spirits of righteous men made perfect, to Jesus the mediator of a new covenant, and to the sprinkled blood that speaks a better word than the blood of Abel.*

Many in the church believe that they have arrived and passed this point. However, in reality many have never arrived at Pentecost. But more than that: Many who have come to Pentecost are no different than the Israelites when they arrived at mount Sinai. We read that they were afraid and settled to have Moses represent them, as described in Exodus 20:18-20:

> *When the people saw the thunder and lightning and heard the trumpet and saw the mountain in smoke, they trembled with fear. They stayed at a distance and said to Moses, "Speak to us yourself and we will listen. But do not have God speak to us or we will die."*
>
> *Moses said to the people, "Do not be afraid. God has come to test you, so that the fear of God will be with you to keep you from sinning."*
>
> *The people remained at a distance, while Moses approached the thick darkness where God was.*

The picture in the church is not much different today. There are many who are literally scared to allow the Holy Spirit to move in the church. They would rather settle for a powerless gospel and rationalize that the gifts of the Spirit are not valid for today and are afraid of opening the door to the Spirit. They fear Pentecost as Israel feared Sinai. Others who have seen the power and presence of the Spirit have chosen to let "the anointed leaders" enter into the presence of God for them and minister to them and on their behalf. Thus, in most churches we have maintained the Aaronic priesthood that was instituted by Emperor Constantine - even within the Pentecostal churches.

In addition to this, those of us that have been open to the Spirit, have failed to see the connection with the law. In many charismatic circles (and also other traditions) we have developed a theology that minimizes and throws away the law. Without going into detail here, we need to note that Jesus did not come to abolish the law of God, but to fulfill it. The Spirit was given to enable us to live according to God's plan and purpose. Let me illustrate this from Romans 6:17-18 and Matthew 7:21-27. Just read these and listen to the Spirit, while recognizing that the outpouring of the Spirit on Pentecost changed the letter of the law and any legalism by writing the law in the heart of each believer (as we shall shortly discuss).

But thanks be to God that, though you used to be slaves to sin, you wholeheartedly obeyed the form of teaching to which you were entrusted. You have been set free from sin and have become slaves to righteousness.

"Not everyone who says to me, `Lord, Lord,' will enter the kingdom of heaven, but only he who does the will of my Father who is in heaven. Many will say to me on that day, `Lord, Lord, did we not prophesy in your name, and in your name drive out demons and perform many miracles?' Then I will tell them plainly, `I never knew you. Away from me, you evildoers!'"

"Therefore, everyone who hears these words of mine and puts them into practice is like a wise man who built his house on the rock. The rain came down, the streams rose, and the winds blew and beat against that house; yet it did not fall, because it had its foundation on the rock. But everyone who hears these words of mine and does not put them into practice is like a foolish man

who built his house on sand. The rain came down, the streams rose, and the winds blew and beat against that house, and it fell with a great crash."

In this third day our Lord is calling us through the gate to move outside into the wilderness where he will restore us and perfect us as his body. In Christ God made a new covenant with us and sealed it with his blood. As we move into the wilderness, willing to suffer disgrace and persecution for his sake, he promised to meet us and perfect us. The church needs to be restored to its foundations and built upon the Rock according to the new covenant. Now we read about this covenant and the work of the Spirit in this regard in Hebrews 8:6-13:

But in fact, the ministry Jesus has received is as superior to theirs as the covenant of which he is mediator is superior to the old one, since the new covenant is established on better promises.
For if there had been nothing wrong with that first covenant, no place would have been sought for another.
But God found fault with the people and said:

"The time is coming, declares the Lord,
when I will make a new covenant with the house of Israel
and with the house of Judah.
It will not be like the covenant I made with their forefathers
when I took them by the hand to lead them out of Egypt,
because they did not remain faithful to my covenant,
and I turned away from them, declares the Lord.

<u>This is the covenant I will make with the house of Israel after that time,</u>

declares the Lord.
I will put my laws in their minds and write them on their hearts.
I will be their God, and they will be my people.
No longer will a man teach his neighbor,
or a man his brother, saying, 'Know the Lord,'
because they will all know me, from the least of them to the
greatest.
For I will forgive their wickedness and will remember their sins
no more."

By calling this covenant "new," he has made the first one obsolete;
and what is obsolete and aging will soon disappear.

God's purpose for each person on this planet is to know him intimately and to live his/her life fully within the will of God. Pentecost is the down payment of the Spirit for those who respond in faith to the call of God. Through the Spirit we can know the will of God for our lives. We do not need someone else to teach us (see 1 John 2:27). That was part of the old covenant with its Levitical order, which has become obsolete with the new covenant in Christ. These are foundational issues that believers ought to know, but because the church structure is a Levitical model, few do and most rely on "the anointed" leaders to do the ministry for them and to teach them. We have built our churches on wrong foundations using a man-made copy of the old obsolete plans and the cracks are showing more and more. Combining the pictures of Hosea 6:3 and Matthew 7:26-27 as God releases the refreshing rains of his Spirit in this third day, many a building will fall down for the foundations were built on sand. This is the very same message Jesus spoke using the picture of the new wine and new garment in Luke 5:36-39:

> *He told them this parable: "No one tears a patch from a new garment and sews it on an old one. If he does, he will have torn the new garment, and the patch from the new will not match the old. And no one pours new wine into old wineskins. If he does, the new wine will burst the skins, the wine will run out and the wineskins will be ruined. No, new wine must be poured into new wineskins. And no one after drinking old wine wants the new, for he says, `The old is better.'"*

If we consider that the former rain of the day of Pentecost, which was but a deposit of the full manifestation of the latter rain, literally tore apart the wineskin of the old Levitical order, then the same will inevitably happen with the revised Christianized Levitical church when the latter rain starts to fall. The sad fact is that much of the new garment of revelation truth revealed by the Spirit to the body is being cut up to patch the old garment, e.g. the emphasis on mega churches and buildings with a Levitical hierarchy as model of how the five-fold ministry is to operate. In this beginning of the third day, God is calling his people out through these gates into the desert. He is calling his bride into the desert as we read in Hosea 2:14-20. There he will speak tenderly to her and betroth her forever. He is seeking a remnant that will be willing to learn obedience through suffering and will pay the price to tabernacle in the wilderness and seek him. He is seeking those who will allow him to cut open their hearts and write his law deep inside their being. He is calling out a people who will again walk in humility and submit to his will, even if it cost them everything.

Why the desert? Why the wilderness? Why outside of the structure of the Western church? It is very simple: That is where the harvest is to be gathered. He is more concerned about the ninety-nine outside than the one inside – for our wrong structure has meant that the vast majority are outside and do not know our Lord. We have been so concerned about our buildings and programs that we have forgotten our mission. Many of us inside do not even know our Lord, for we do not know his heartbeat for the lost. We need to return to our first love again. He is calling us into the wilderness to meet us and to reveal himself to us as he promised in Hosea 6:1-3.

<u>The third day is foreshadowed in the feast of Tabernacles when the church will move out into the wilderness and live in temporary shelters in order to gather the harvest.</u> However, before we can gather the harvest, we need to be prepared. We will never gather the harvest without knowing the heart of God for the lost. Our Lord is calling us out through the gate, because we need to get away from our own agendas and programs. Most of the mission and outreach of the church in our society is done to build our own little Levitical kingdoms. That is why most new churches in our society are built simply by gathering sheep from another's field. Our church growth is mostly at the expense of other churches. God

is calling his remnant out to meet him in the wilderness and to tabernacle with him. We need open-heart surgery in which he can write his law in our hearts so that we truly love him with all our heart and mind and strength and our neighbor as we love ourselves. We need to get the mind of Christ and learn to walk in obedience as he did. We need to be perfected as his body on earth.

In the wilderness we will be tempted and tested as he was. Like our Lord, the devil will put us to the test. As we step out of the nice structure of our comfort zones in our churches, we will face opposition we have never known. In a very real way, we will need to trust God for provision. This is not just for members of the Levitical order who walk away from the support and income of the religious structure (and I know that from personal experience). It will be for all who will obey the law of God written in their hearts, e.g. the doctor who refuses to kill the unborn or the teacher who will teach the truth in the classroom. Will we be tempted by the hunger of our need for bread or choose to go hungry and be a living stone being shaped and placed in the eternal temple? Likewise, we will face the temptation of power and authority to rule over kingdoms. It may be as simple as control over a spouse or children, but it will face us. For some of us the first step into the wilderness is to deal with the control issues in our lives. <u>The root of the Levitical order in most churches is the spirit of control and God is calling us out through the gate.</u> We will either serve God and worship him alone in Spirit and in truth or we will worship the devil. Like our Lord, we will also be tempted to misuse the gifts, power and authority given to us in Christ for our own selfish ends and put God to the test. The church has a sad history of misusing God's grace and gifts and no one is exempt. From another angle, God will deal with these things in our lives on different levels – personal, corporate and national. No one of us is an island upon himself and God calls us into the wilderness to prepare us for the work of ministry.

It is in the desert that we will find not only our God, but also the harvest to be gathered. It is precisely in the wastelands of our societies that the harvest is ripening. It is where the need is greatest that we will find hearts open to hear the good news. This is why the kingdom of God always advances where there is opposition and persecution. The ones who are thirsty come to the water. Now, it is very interesting to note that the only Biblical reference we have about Jesus attending the feast of Tabernacles is in John 7:37- 39 where we read:

> *On the last and greatest day of the Feast, Jesus stood and said in a loud voice, "If anyone is thirsty, let him come to me and drink. Whoever believes in me, as the Scripture has said, streams of living water will flow from within him." By this he meant the Spirit, whom those who believed in him were later to receive. Up to that time the Spirit had not been given, since Jesus had not yet been glorified.*

Listen, it was in the very wasteland of Samaria that Jesus sat at the well at noon and from the innermost being of one lonely and rejected woman, came a well of living water that transformed a whole community. However, the disciples were so concerned about their daily bread that Jesus had to point out to them that the fields are ripe for the harvest. Read again for yourselves John 4:16-43:

> *Just then his disciples returned and were surprised to find him talking with a woman. But no one asked, "What do you want?" or "Why are you talking with her?"*

> *Then, leaving her water jar, the woman went back to the town and said to the people, "Come, see a man who told me everything I ever did. Could this be the Christ?" They came out of the town and made their way toward him.*

> *Meanwhile his disciples urged him, "Rabbi, eat something." But he said to them, "I have food to eat that you know nothing about." Then his disciples said to each other, "Could someone have brought him food?"*

"My food," said Jesus, "is to do the will of him who sent me and to finish his work. Do you not say, `Four months more and then the harvest'? I tell you, open your eyes and look at the fields! They are ripe for harvest. Even now the reaper draws his wages, even now he harvests the crop for eternal life, so that the sower and the reaper may be glad together. Thus the saying `One sows and another reaps' is true. I sent you to reap what you have not worked for. Others have done the hard work, and you have reaped the benefits of their labor."

Many of the Samaritans from that town believed in him because of the woman's testimony, "He told me everything I ever did." So, when the Samaritans came to him, they urged him to stay with them, and he stayed two days. And because of his words many more became believers. They said to the woman, "We no longer believe just because of what you said; now we have heard for ourselves, and we know that this man really is the Savior of the world.

In fact, not long after that, the church reaped a mighty harvest in those same fields when Philip took the message to these rejected people (see Acts 8) in obedience to the word of the Lord in Acts 1:8:

But you will receive power when the Holy Spirit comes on you; and you will be my witnesses in Jerusalem, and in all Judea <u>and Samaria</u>, and to the ends of the earth.

As Michael Wood would say: "In case you think I am repeating myself, let me say it again: The church was never called to be institutionalized and to be inside the walls of a building called 'a church.'" The church is to be the salt of the earth – outside and in the world. We are to seek those outside and meet their needs. The prophetic word in Isaiah 41:17-20 reads:

<u>The poor and needy search for water,</u>
<u>but there is none;</u>
<u>their tongues are parched with thirst.</u>

<u>But I the LORD will answer them,</u>
<u>I, the God of Israel, will not forsake them.</u>

<u>I will make rivers flow on barren heights,</u>
<u>and springs within the valleys.</u>

I will turn the desert into pools of water,
and the parched ground into springs.
I will put in the desert the cedar and the acacia,
the myrtle and the olive.
I will set pines in the wasteland, the fir and the cypress together,
so that people may see and know, may consider and understand
that the hand of the LORD has done this,
that the Holy One of Israel has created it.

Those of us who have tasted the rain of Pentecost, have within us the very water that can quench the thirst of those in the desert. As we enter the world in his name and as our hearts beat with the compassion of our Lord, from within are released rivers of living water. Listen to the prophetic promise of Isaiah 35:

The desert and the parched land will be glad;
the wilderness will rejoice and blossom.
Like the crocus, it will burst into bloom;
it will rejoice greatly and shout for joy.
The glory of Lebanon will be given to it,
the splendor of Carmel and Sharon;
they will see the glory of the LORD,
the splendor of our God.

Strengthen the feeble hands,
steady the knees that give way
say to those with fearful hearts,
"Be strong, do not fear; your God will come,
he will come with vengeance;
with divine retribution
he will come to save you."

Then will the eyes of the blind be opened
and the ears of the deaf unstopped.
Then will the lame leap like a deer,
and the mute tongue shout for joy.
Water will gush forth in the wilderness
and streams in the desert.

The burning sand will become a pool,
the thirsty ground bubbling springs.
In the haunts where jackals once lay,
grass and reeds and papyrus will grow.

And a highway will be there;
it will be called the Way of Holiness.
The unclean will not journey on it;
it will be for those who walk in that Way;
wicked fools will not go about on it.
No lion will be there, nor will any ferocious beast get up on it;
they will not be found there.

But only the redeemed will walk there,
and the ransomed of the LORD will return.
They will enter Zion with singing;
everlasting joy will crown their heads.
Gladness and joy will overtake them,
and sorrow and sighing will flee away.

This is the prophetic promise of the harvest to be gathered in this third day of our Lord. He is calling us into the desert to restore, equip and release us to do the work reserved for this generation. As we tabernacle with him, we are changed by his very presence and his glory is seen in us as we are revealed as the sons of God.

THE REVELATION OF THE SONS OF GOD

In the third day Jesus will perfect his body, the church. Every member individually will be perfected and will perfectly function in his/her specific place in the body. At this point in history, we are in the process of moving to that place and as we have seen, we are called out of the Levitical structures, through the gate, into the place where each one will tabernacle with the Lord. It is in the place of personal and corporate intimacy with our Lord, symbolized by the booths in the wilderness, that we are disciplined as God's sons. Let us read Hebrews 12:5-11:

You have forgotten that word of encouragement that addresses you as sons:

> *"My son, do not make light of the Lord's discipline,*
> *and do not lose heart when he rebukes you,*

because the Lord disciplines those he loves,
and he punishes everyone he accepts as a son."

Endure hardship as discipline; God is treating you as sons. For what son is not disciplined by his father? If you are not disciplined (and everyone undergoes discipline), then you are illegitimate children and not true sons. Moreover, we have all had human fathers who disciplined us and we respected them for it. How much more should we submit to the Father of our spirits and live! Our fathers disciplined us for a little while as they thought best; but God disciplines us for our good, that we may share in his holiness. No discipline seems pleasant at the time, but painful. Later on, however, it produces a harvest of righteousness and peace for those who have been trained by it.

Much earlier in the book we saw that we were divinely appointed to overcome the enemy and make him a footstool for our Lord. The first step in the process is to overcome sin in our lives and to live by the Spirit. We have become sons of God and need to learn how to live as sons. This is the very heart of Paul's message in Romans 8 where he talks about the law of the Spirit of life that has set us free from the law of sin and death. He continues in Romans 8:12-17:

Therefore, brothers, we have an obligation - but it is not to the sinful nature, to live according to it. For if you live according to the sinful nature, you will die; but if by the Spirit you put to death the misdeeds of the body, you will live, <u>because those who are led by the Spirit of God are sons of God. For you did not receive a spirit that makes you a slave again to fear, but you received the Spirit of sonship. And by him we cry, "Abba, Father." The Spirit himself</u>

testifies with our spirit that we are God's children. Now if we are children, then we are heirs - heirs of God and co-heirs with Christ, if indeed we share in his sufferings in order that we may also share in his glory.

Note that as we move out into the presence of God, because we are sons, we do not walk in fear. In the words of Hebrews 4:16 we enter into his presence with confidence. We know that we have not come to a mountain that cannot be touched as we read in Hebrews 12:18-25:

You have not come to a mountain that can be touched and that is burning with fire; to darkness, gloom and storm; to a trumpet blast or to such a voice speaking words that those who heard it begged that no further word be spoken to them, because they could not bear what was commanded: "If even an animal touches the mountain, it must be stoned." The sight was so terrifying that Moses said, "I am trembling with fear."

But you have come to Mount Zion, to the heavenly Jerusalem, the city of the living God. You have come to thousands upon thousands of angels in joyful assembly, to the church of the firstborn, whose names are written in heaven. You have come to God, the judge of all men, to the spirits of righteous men made perfect, to Jesus the mediator of a new covenant, and to the sprinkled blood that speaks a better word than the blood of Abel.

See to it that you do not refuse him who speaks.

In Christ God became our Father and we cry "Abba, Father." As children we have become heirs of God and co-heirs with Christ. Those who understand this are willing to step through the gate and suffer the disgrace he bore, for they know that if they share in his suffering, they shall also share in his glory! Thus, they are willing to be disciplined by the Father in order that they may be perfected as sons as they learn obedience through suffering. They are willing to hear his voice and walk in obedience. They are willing to be disciplined to walk in the order of Melchizedek and to be a kingdom of priests. They are like Paul who *considered everything a loss compared to the surpassing greatness of knowing Christ Jesus his Lord, for whose sake he has lost all things. He considered them rubbish that he may gain Christ and be found in him, not having a righteousness of his own that comes from the law, but that which is through faith in Christ - the righteousness that comes from God and is by faith. He wanted to know Christ and the power of his resurrection and the fellowship of sharing in his sufferings, becoming like him in his death, and so, somehow, to attain to the resurrection from the dead.* (Philippians 3:8-11).

Those who walk out through the gate, willing to share in suffering and to be disciplined by the Father, know the words of Paul in Romans 8:18-30:

I consider that our present sufferings are not worth comparing with the glory that will be revealed in us. The creation waits in eager expectation for the sons of God to be revealed. For the creation was subjected to frustration, not by its own choice, but by the will of the one who subjected it, in hope that the creation itself will be liberated from its bondage to decay and brought into the glorious freedom of the children of God.

We know that the whole creation has been groaning as in the pains of childbirth right up to the present time. Not only so, but <u>we ourselves, who have the first fruits of the Spirit, groan inwardly as we wait eagerly for our adoption as sons, the redemption of our bodies.</u> For in this hope we were saved. But hope that is seen is no hope at all. Who hopes for what he already has? But if we hope for what we do not yet have, we wait for it patiently.

In the same way, the Spirit helps us in our weakness. We do not know what we ought to pray for, but the Spirit himself intercedes for us with groans that words cannot express. And he who searches our hearts knows the mind of the Spirit, because the Spirit intercedes for the saints in accordance with God's will.

<u>And we know that in all things God works for the good of those who love him, who have been called according to his purpose. For those God foreknew, he also predestined to be conformed to the likeness of his Son, that he might be the firstborn among many brothers. And those he predestined, he also called; those he called, he also justified; those he justified, he also glorified.</u>

When God calls us out into the wilderness to tabernacle with him and be in his presence, it is a step towards our maturity as sons. The whole creation is pregnant with expectation to see the revelation of the sons of God. To understand this, we need to look at the three pilgrimage festivals and their meaning again. Our Passover is the remembrance of our salvation experience and water baptism. It is when we are born again into the kingdom of God! We are born again by the Spirit as Jesus explained to Nicodemus in John 3:5-8. At that moment the new believer becomes a child of God. However, just as in the natural the newborn needs to be fed with milk. As we saw earlier, within many of the churches most never move beyond this stage. Like the Hebrews they struggle to understand the order of Melchizedek because they are slow to learn and prefer milk to solid food (Hebrews 5:11-14).

As Israel moved from Passover and the Red Sea deliverance they came to Sinai where the Lord appeared and they received the blueprint for their lives and mission. This was their Pentecost experience and later became the symbol of the first fruits of the harvest. As we have seen they were afraid of the Lord and chose to have Moses represent them. They thus chose not to enter into the order of Melchizedek, but to have the order of Levi. Even so, the Lord allowed them to tabernacle and to mature as his people – and those that refused and rebelled died in the wilderness. This was later remembered in the feast of Tabernacles and the gathering of the harvest. For us in the new covenant, Pentecost represents the time of the outpouring of the Spirit to equip us for our mission. The Spirit is poured upon us and fills us. The Spirit writes the law in our hearts to guide us as we grow up as sons and begin to take responsibility for our spiritual lives. In a very real way, Pentecost is the time when a young boy in Jewish culture celebrates his Bar Mitzvah. He is now able to take responsibility, to be trained, to become fully responsible. From that moment he walks with his father and shares in the business as co-worker. This is where the discipline and training of the father really brings the changes to maturity. In the words of Paul in Romans 8:23 we who have the first fruits (that is have experienced the Pentecost of the Holy Spirit's baptism) groan inwardly as we await our adoption as sons. The word translated as "adoption" is the technical term when a son is released to take a full position in the family business. This is represented in the feast of Tabernacles. There is a time coming when we will be mature in Christ.

In a very real sense, every believer is in process from spiritual infancy through adolescence to adulthood. Some choose to remain infants or adolescents. They do not want to grow beyond that stage and in reality, the structure of the church, as we know it, functions to keep the majority in the stage of infants. Some progress beyond that and become rebellious spiritual teenagers. One of the greatest problems in the church is that there is a lack of spiritual fathers, like Paul who could appeal to a rebellious body of believers as a father and who fathered many leaders like Timothy, e.g. 1 Corinthians 4:14-17:

I am not writing this to shame you, but to warn you, as my dear children. Even though you have ten thousand guardians in Christ, you do not have many fathers, for in Christ Jesus I became your father through the gospel. Therefore, I urge you to imitate me. For this reason, I am sending to you Timothy, my son whom I love, who is faithful in the Lord. He will remind you of my way of life in Christ Jesus, which agrees with what I teach everywhere in every church.

This is really the key reason for the appointment of the fivefold ministry gifts. God gave the apostles, prophets, evangelists, pastors and teachers to equip the members of the body for their work. Their task is not to rule and reign, but to perfect the others for their work of service. Having done that, like Paul did with Timothy, they are to release them into ministry. However, our churches are run by guardians of tradition and there is a lack of fathers. We need leaders who could groan in the Spirit like Paul when he wrote to Galatians 4:19: *My dear children, for whom I am again in the pains of childbirth until Christ is formed in you.*

As we begin this third day in the Lord, we are called to move outside of the walls into the place of intimacy where we can be disciplined and grow to maturity. It is both as individuals and also on the corporate level. We need to spend time with God and allow him to change what needs to be changed in us. The first fruits of Pentecost which was the deposit guaranteeing the future promise, must be perfected. We need to learn to relate to the Father and to hear the voice of the Lord. We need to learn how to walk in the Spirit. In the words of Galatians 4:19 Christ must be formed in each of us. As we have seen Christ went through the gate and suffered outside and so we are called out to bear the disgrace he bore and be made holy (Hebrews 13:13). In the words of the apostle Peter:

Therefore, rid yourselves of all malice and all deceit, hypocrisy, envy, and slander of every kind. Like newborn babies, crave pure spiritual milk, so that by it you may grow up in your salvation, now that you have tasted that the Lord is good.

As you come to him, the living Stone - rejected by men but chosen by God and precious to him - you also, like living stones, are being built into a spiritual house to be a holy priesthood, offering spiritual sacrifices acceptable to God through Jesus Christ. For in Scripture it says:

"See, I lay a stone in Zion,
a chosen and precious cornerstone,
and the one who trusts in him will never be put to shame."

Now to you who believe, this stone is precious.
But to those who do not believe,

"The stone the builders rejected has become the capstone,"
and,
"A stone that causes men to stumble and a rock that makes them fall."

They stumble because they disobey the message - which is also what they were destined for.
But you are a chosen people, a royal priesthood,
a holy nation, a people belonging to God,
that you may declare the praises of him
who called you out of darkness into his wonderful light.
Once you were not a people, but now you are the people of God;
once you had not received mercy, but now you have received mercy.
(1 Peter 2:1-10).

<u>As we come to him who suffered outside, we are being handled as precious living stones and built into the building of his house where his glory resides.</u> Note that it begins with the idea of us growing up in our salvation and thus moving to maturity. Then follows the picture of the building and like Hebrews 13:13 the focus is on the rejection and suffering of Jesus through which he became the cornerstone. Having worked with buildings and watched stone masons work, stones have to be shaped – and it involves chipping away pieces. Likewise, we are to go through testing and shaping as God is building us together into this spiritual house to be a holy priesthood – in the order of Melchizedek our High Priest.

<u>It is in this stepping out to be associated with him who was rejected for our sake that we find God working out all things for good for us.</u> It is in the willingness to be conformed to the likeness of his Son that we are changed and our lives begin to move in the direction of his call and purpose (Romans 8:28-30). As we step away from all the man- made structures and schemes, however religious, we find the way into the Most Holy Place revealed to us (Hebrews 9:8) and we experience the tremendous love of God and become more than conquerors. This is what Paul explained in Romans 8:31-39:

What, then, shall we say in response to this? If God is for us, who can be against us? He who did not spare his own Son, but gave him up for us all - how will he not also, along with him, graciously give us all things? Who will bring any charge against those whom God has chosen? It is God who justifies. Who is he that condemns? Christ Jesus, who died - more than that, who was raised to life-is at the right hand of God and is also interceding for us. Who shall separate us from the love of Christ? Shall trouble or hardship or persecution or famine or nakedness or danger or sword? As it is written:

"For your sake we face death all day long; we are considered as sheep to be slaughtered."

No, in all these things we are more than conquerors through him who loved us. For I am convinced that neither death nor life, neither angels nor demons, neither the present nor the future, nor any powers, neither height nor depth, nor anything else in all creation, will be able to separate us from the love of God that is in Christ Jesus our Lord.

Note again that the victory comes amidst all kinds of trials and persecutions and troubles. What we can count on is the absolute certainty of God's love for us. As we face these things, we become more than conquerors and the enemy is brought under the feet of our High Priest who is seated at the right hand of the Father.

<u>As priests in the order of Melchizedek we follow the example of our eternal High Priest. As he offered himself as sacrifice on the cross, so are we to take up our cross and follow him. As he gave his body, so are we to offer our bodies as living sacrifices, holy and pleasing to God.</u> It is in the place of daily being in the presence of the Lord, symbolized in living in booths every day

of the week (seven full days) that the image of Christ begins to take shape in us. It is by moving out of the man- made structures built on the Levitical foundations, that we are able to see the way into the Most Holy Place and be in that place seven days a week, regardless of our circumstances. That is the place where we enter into the Sabbath rest and we are no longer striving to serve and please God, but we begin to walk in the call and purpose for our lives. We *have been transformed by the renewal of our minds and are able to test and approve the perfect will of God* (Romans 12:2) *and we make every effort to enter into the rest for the people of God, not following the example of disobedience* (Hebrews 4:11).

God is calling us into this place of his presence and those who are willing to enter into that place of intimacy, will get pregnant with the plans and purposes of God. It is in this place that the living Word, which is sharper than a double-edged sword, cuts through the division between soul and spirit and the veil separating the two, is torn (Hebrews 4:12). The living Word is able to move freely from our spirit into our minds, which are transformed and our spiritual eyes are opened to know the hope to which we were called and <u>the riches of his glorious inheritance in the saints</u> and his incomparably great power for us who believe (Ephesians 1:18-19).

As each individual walks into the Most Holy Place to be transformed and perfected by walking and living in obedience, testing and approving the perfect will of God, we are shaped and being placed as living stones in this spiritual house. In this process we are brought into relationship with one another where each one has his specific role and function as Paul described in Romans 12 and 1 Corinthians 12 and Ephesians 4. However, there is a very important issue to note in this process and the New Testament speaks of this in many passages, e.g. Romans 12:3-21:

For by the grace given me I say to every one of you: Do not think of yourself more highly than you ought, but rather think of yourself with sober judgment, in accordance with the measure of faith God has given you. Just as each of us has one body with many members, and these members do not all have the same function, so in Christ we who are many form one body, and each member belongs to all the others. We have different gifts, according to the grace given us. If a man's gift is prophesying, let him use it in proportion to his faith. If it is serving, let him serve; if it is teaching, let him teach; if it is encouraging, let him encourage; if it is contributing to the needs of others, let him give generously; if it is leadership, let him govern diligently; if it is showing mercy, let him do it cheerfully.

Love must be sincere. Hate what is evil; cling to what is good. Be devoted to one another in brotherly love. Honor one another above yourselves. Never be lacking in zeal, but keep your spiritual fervor, serving the Lord. Be joyful in hope, patient in affliction, faithful in prayer. Share with God's people who are in need. Practice hospitality.

Bless those who persecute you; bless and do not curse. Rejoice with those who rejoice; mourn with those who mourn. Live in harmony *with one another. <u>Do not be proud, but be willing to associate with people of low position. Do not be conceited.</u>*

Do not repay anyone evil for evil. Be careful to do what is right in the eyes of everybody. If it is possible, as far as it depends on you, live at peace with everyone. Do not take revenge, my friends, but leave room for God's wrath, for it is written: "It is mine to avenge; I will repay," says the Lord. On the contrary:

> *"If your enemy is hungry, feed him;*
> *if he is thirsty, give him something to drink.*
> *In doing this, you will heap burning coals on his head."*

Do not be overcome by evil, but overcome evil with good.

One of the reasons that God is calling us out of the Levitical structures of our churches is precisely because the hierarchical structure of these churches is a radical departure from the order of Melchizedek where greatness is shown in becoming a servant, as our High Priest said and showed by his example, e.g. Matthew 20:25-28:

Jesus called them together and said, "You know that the rulers of the Gentiles lord it over them, and their high officials exercise authority over them. Not so with you. Instead, whoever wants to become great among you must be your servant, and whoever wants to be first must be your slave - just as the Son of Man did not come to be served, but to serve, and to give his life as a ransom for many."

It is in this way of life that the royal authority is released to the body, called the church. It is radically different from the worldly models. This is why the leaders in the church, particularly those given as gifts in the five-fold ministry, are to be servants equipping and releasing those whom they serve. The third day church is a body of ordinary people, walking in royal authority, serving one another and the world in sacrificial ways with radical authenticity. They live and walk in the presence of God seven days a week and need no special buildings, titles or man-made structure to experience the presence and power of God. They are not driven, but rest in the Lord and know how and when to respond to the needs around them. They touch and influence the world for they are comfortable being the body of Christ in the world and through them the Word of God is made flesh. In the words of Paul in 2 Corinthians 4:5-11:

For we do not preach ourselves, but Jesus Christ as Lord, and ourselves as your servants for Jesus' sake. For God, who said, "Let light shine out of darkness," made his light shine in our hearts to give us the light of the knowledge of the glory of God in the face of Christ.

But we have this treasure in jars of clay to show that this all-surpassing power is from God and not from us. We are hard pressed on every side, but not crushed; perplexed, but not in despair; persecuted, but not abandoned; struck down, but not destroyed. We always carry around in our body the death of Jesus, so that the life of Jesus may also be revealed in our body. For we who are alive are always being given over to death for Jesus' sake, so that his life may be revealed in our mortal body.

In this third day, God is constructing his house where his glory will be revealed like never before. He began with the stone that the builders rejected and made that into the cornerstone. He laid the foundations using the least likely stones: fishermen, tax collectors, "doubtful Tom" and even a learned scholar whose life was changed in the dust road to Damascus and a Levite by the name of Barnabus. In the first layers of this house of God he had no problem to include a Mary Magdalene or people from Corinth to whom Paul wrote (1 Corinthians 1:26-30):

Brothers, think of what you were when you were called. Not many of you were wise by human standards; not many were influential; not many were of noble birth. But God chose the foolish things of the world to shame the wise; God chose the weak things of the world to shame the strong. He chose the lowly things of this world and the despised things - and the things that are not - to nullify the things that are, so that no one may boast before him. It is because of him that you are in Christ Jesus, who has become for us wisdom from God - that is, our righteousness, holiness and redemption. Therefore, as it is written: "Let him who boasts boast in the Lord."

To this day God is doing the same. He is still calling the most unlikely ones and as they grasp the message of the cross and walk out through the gate into the world, they become the very instruments of his grace and power. The house that he is perfecting in this third day is the house that will reveal his glory and is not build by human hands with bricks and mortar. It is a spiritual house in which ordinary people will serve as holy priests, bringing spiritual sacrifices to God through our High Priest Jesus Christ. They are a chosen people, royal priests and a holy nation, declaring the praises of him who called them out of darkness into his marvelous light. This is the house that will remain standing when the heavens and the earth are shaken and the glory of God revealed, as we shall see next.

THE KINGDOM THAT CANNOT BE SHAKEN

There is a time in the future when God will shake the heavens and the earth. In Hebrews 12:18-24 the author contrasted the old and the new covenant. The first took place at Mount Sinai where Israel was gathered in fear and trembling. Then we read that we have come to Mount Zion and the new covenant in Christ, which is far better. Then he continues in Hebrews 12:25-29:

See to it that you do not refuse him who speaks. If they did not escape when they refused him who warned them on earth, how much less will we, if we turn away from him who warns us from heaven? At that time his voice shook the earth, but now he has promised, "Once more I will shake not only the earth but also the heavens." The words "once more" indicate the removing of what can be shaken - that is, created things - so that what cannot be shaken may remain.

Therefore, since we are receiving a kingdom that cannot be shaken, let us be thankful, and so worship God acceptably with reverence and awe, for our "God is a consuming fire."

As we move into this third day of the church more and more people are looking at the signs of the times. This is not the place to go into the details of the end times, but it is more than interesting to read some of the words Jesus spoke to his disciples about the signs, e.g. Luke 21:5-19:

Some of his disciples were remarking about how the temple was adorned with beautiful stones and with gifts dedicated to God. But Jesus said, "As for what you see here, the time will come when not one stone will be left on another; every one of them will be thrown down."

"Teacher," they asked, "when will these things happen? <u>And what will be the sign that they are about to take place?"</u>

He replied: "Watch out that you are not deceived. For many will come in my name, claiming, `I am he,' and, `the time is near.' Do not follow them. When you hear of wars and revolutions, do not be frightened. These things must happen first, but the end will not come right away."

<u>*Then he said to them: "Nation will rise against nation, and kingdom against kingdom. There will be great earthquakes, famines and pestilences in various places, and fearful events and great signs from heaven.*</u>

<u>*But before all this, they will lay hands on you and persecute you. They will deliver you to synagogues and prisons, and you will be*</u>

brought before kings and governors, and all on account of my name. This will result in your being witnesses to them. But make up your mind not to worry beforehand how you will defend yourselves. For I will give you words and wisdom that none of your adversaries will be able to resist or contradict. You will be betrayed even by parents, brothers, relatives and friends, and they will put some of you to death. All men will hate you because of me. But not a hair of your head will perish. By standing firm you will gain life.

No matter how we want to interpret these signs, they all indicate that there will be much shaking and instability during the end times. The worst spot to be when this happens is in a building that cannot withstand the shaking and will collapse. This is why there are special building codes in areas that frequently experience earthquakes so that the buildings will not easily collapse. In the same way the Scriptures have specific spiritual building codes that will allow the structures to withstand the coming shaking of the heavens and the earth. Nothing that is of human origin will remain (Hebrews 12:27). This is why we are called out of the city through the gate to tabernacle in booths! Ultimately that is the place of safety and security, for then we are under the shadow of his wings (Psalm 91). Jesus said we should first seek the kingdom of God and his righteousness and the rest will fall in place. This is the kingdom that cannot be shaken and will remain into eternity. To put it in other words, we are to invest our lives in kingdom ventures, for all that are man-made and of human origin will not last.

It is more than coincidence that the quote in Hebrews 12:26 is from a passage in the Old Testament dealing with the rebuilding of the temple that was destroyed by Nebuchadnezzar when Jerusalem fell to the Babylonians. Those who returned from the exile, after Cyrus had conquered Babylon, were a small remnant and most had little financial means. They started the rebuilding, but quit, as the task seemed beyond their means. Then God used the prophets Haggai and Zechariah to challenge them to make this their priority. Let us read Haggai 2:1-9:

On the twenty-first day of the seventh month, the word of the LORD came through the prophet Haggai: "Speak to Zerubbabel son of Shealtiel, governor of Judah, to Joshua son of Jehozadak, the high priest, and to the remnant of the people. Ask them, `who of you is left who saw this house in its former glory? How does it look to you now? Does it not seem to you like nothing? But now be strong, O Zerubbabel,' declares the LORD. `Be strong, O Joshua son of Jehozadak, the high priest. Be strong, all you people of the land,' declares the LORD, `and work. For I am with you,' declares the LORD Almighty.

`This is what I covenanted with you when you came out of Egypt. And my Spirit remains among you. Do not fear.'

"This is what the LORD Almighty says: `In a little while I will once more shake the heavens and the earth, the sea and the dry land. I will shake all nations, and the desired of all nations will come, and I will fill this house with glory,' says the LORD Almighty. `The silver is mine and the gold is mine,' declares the LORD Almighty. `The glory of this present house will be greater

than the glory of the former house,' says the LORD Almighty. 'And in this place I will grant peace,' declares the LORD Almighty."

Today the church of God in our part of the world needs to be restored and rebuilt from the foundations up. It is a matter of priorities. We have beautiful buildings with all the modern equipment to run all the programs. We have pulpits and altars and communion tables – but we miss the glory! The man-made structures and programs do not satisfy. It was little different in Jesus' day. He visited a magnificent temple where priests and Levites served at the altar, but it made no difference to the lives of people. When he came to his own people, they did not recognize him. Jerusalem missed the day of its visitation. Those who knew the Scriptures did not recognize God when he himself stepped into their midst. When the glory entered the temple, they did not see it, for they were too busy with their own kingdoms and their pyramids of importance. <u>But those outside recognized the glory and so lepers were cleansed, blind eyes saw him, deaf ears were opened, captives were set free and the poor heard the good news!</u>

He looked and saw the multitudes that were like sheep without a shepherd. He had compassion upon them! He saw many tired and burdened, carrying the heavy religious loads placed upon them and he called them (Matthew 11:28-30):

"Come to me, all you who are weary and burdened, and I will give you rest. Take my yoke upon you and learn from me, for I am

gentle and humble in heart, and you will find rest for your souls. For my yoke is easy and my burden is light."

Those who came saw the glory and found the rest. Ordinary people discovered their eternal roots before the foundation of the earth and with that found that their lives had divine purposes in him. Fishermen by the names of Peter and John reached out in the name of Jesus and a man crippled from birth was instantly healed. When questioned, they shared the story with the religious leaders despite threats of persecution and then we read (Acts 4:13-14):

<u>When they saw the courage of Peter and John and realized that they were unschooled, ordinary men, they were astonished and they took note that these men had been with Jesus. But since they could see the man who had been healed standing there with them, there was nothing they could say.</u>

In this third day God is rebuilding the church from the foundation up. He is doing it with ordinary men and women who have the courage to walk out and bear the disgrace he bore. He is calling those who are tired of carrying the loads placed upon them by religious leaders and denominational structures to move out through the gate into the world and tabernacle with him. He is calling forth a remnant willing to walk with his kingdom vision and proclaim that in word and in deed. He is anointing and empowering those foolish enough to lay hands on the sick and drive out demons to actually change lives. He even shows up in homes or wherever two or three are gathered in his name and his glory fills the ordinary homes – without stained glass windows, steeples or clergy!

In this third day our Lord is rebuilding his house with living stones. He calls us out of the man-made structures and coverings and traditions into the freedom of the Spirit. What seemed glorious in the man-made Levitical structures has no comparison to the glory revealed in this house. We are able to enter into his presence with boldness. Here every veil and covering are taken away and the glory shines forth in a brilliant radiance as Paul wrote in 2 Corinthians 3:12-18:

Therefore, since we have such a hope, we are very bold. We are not like Moses, who would put a veil over his face to keep the Israelites from gazing at it while the radiance was fading away. But their minds were made dull, for to this day the same veil remains when the old covenant is read. It has not been removed, because only in Christ is it taken away. Even to this day when Moses is read, a veil covers their hearts. But whenever anyone turns to the Lord, the veil is taken away. Now the Lord is the Spirit, and where the Spirit of the Lord is, there is freedom. And we, who with unveiled faces all reflect the Lord's glory, are being transformed into his likeness with ever-increasing glory, which comes from the Lord, who is the Spirit.

Our Lord is calling out those who are willing to pay the price to follow him. He is seeking those who fear him more than man and are willing to give everything for the pearl of great price. He is seeking those who are tired of the empty programs and never-ending projects and the rule of men. He is seeking those who are wandering in the wilderness seeking rest. He is seeking those who are simple enough to trust him and him alone and to take his word seriously. He is seeking those who are willing to be disciplined as sons until they perfectly reflect his glory.

He is seeking leaders who are willing to be servants. He is seeking leaders who truly care about the least. God is seeking leaders that are secure enough to equip and release ordinary people and who can rejoice when they see them exceed beyond their own level. He is seeking leaders who have a vision that is truly his kingdom vision and who will pay the price needed to see it achieved.

This is the house of the Lord, which he is restoring in this third day. In many ways it is no different than the days of Zerubbabel and Haggai. Many who look at the simple beginnings of the house church movement compared to the church, as we have known it for centuries, literally despise the day of small beginnings (Zechariah 4:10). Likewise, the booths in the wilderness did not seem to compare with the magnificence of the temple in Jerusalem. The cross on Calvary did not seem to be the power of God and the wisdom of God. Ordinary housewives and local guys leading meetings in a home without "a right Reverend" and trusting God to show up on a weeknight and even to cover them, do not seem like church to many. <u>But the glory of this latter house will be greater than the glory of the former house!</u> This glory will shine forth in the church and those who understand this will be willing to suffer and die for the truth that every believer is called, anointed and appointed as royal priest in the order of Melchizedek as Paul wrote in Colossians 1:24-27:

Now I rejoice in what was suffered for you, and I fill up in my flesh what is still lacking in regard to Christ's afflictions, for the sake of his body, which is the church. I have become its servant by the commission God gave me to present to you the word of God in its fullness, the mystery that has been kept hidden for ages and generations, but is now disclosed to the saints. To them God has chosen to make known among the Gentiles the glorious riches of this mystery, which is Christ in you, the hope of glory.

It is amazing to realize that after two thousand years this is again a mystery to so many in the church. Like Paul some are literally paying the price for the sake of the body of our Lord, so that this mystery may again be disclosed to the saints. Christ in you is the hope of glory. You are called and sent into the world to make known among those who do not know him the glorious riches of this mystery, which is Christ in you, the hope of glory. You and I do not need any Levitical priest to represent us for we are called to be a royal priesthood in the order of Melchizedek. As believers we have been equipped and anointed for this task as Peter wrote in 2 Peter 1:3-11:

His divine power has given us everything we need for life and godliness through our knowledge of him who called us by his own glory and goodness. Through these he has given us his very great and precious promises, so that through them you may participate in the divine nature and escape the corruption in the world caused by evil desires.

For this very reason, make every effort to add to your faith goodness; and to goodness, knowledge; and to knowledge, self-control; and to self-control, perseverance; and to perseverance, godliness; and to godliness, brotherly kindness; and to brotherly kindness, love. For if you possess these qualities in increasing measure, they will keep you from being ineffective and unproductive in your knowledge of our Lord Jesus Christ. But if anyone does not have them, he is nearsighted and blind, and has forgotten that he has been cleansed from his past sins.

Therefore, my brothers, be all the more eager to make your calling and election sure. For if you do these things, you will never fall, and you will receive a rich welcome into the eternal kingdom of our Lord and Savior Jesus Christ.

Did you notice the last words? When the shaking happens you and I will not be shaken, for we are tied to this his kingdom. We have indeed received an eternal kingdom and we have become a royal priesthood in the order of Melchizedek. That is worth celebrating, wherever we are, seven days a week!

EPILOGUE

Many years ago, God's people ended up in Egypt. It was a place of safety when the famine raged in the Promised Land. They accepted the hospitality and settled. In time things changed and they became slaves to Pharaoh and his followers. In a very real way, the pyramids built during that time represented the very essence of their bondage and oppression. They were the slaves at the bottom of the social structure providing the labor for those at the top who controlled society and had pyramids and palaces built. The pyramids were also magnificent symbols of death and monuments to the grave. But Egypt had the Nile and as a result the comfort of food and water, even for slaves serving the god of death.

On the other side of the Red Sea was a desert wilderness and Mount Sinai on the way to the Promised Land. When they were led to freedom, many never really forgot the food of Egypt. They were ready to return, rather than pay the price of freedom and they eventually died in the wilderness. Even when they were in the Promised Land, they often sought the help of Egypt. More than that: In time, in the promised land, they chose to reject God's rule and they asked for a king like the other nations such as Egypt. They wanted their own Pharaoh and instead of the kingdom of God they ended up with an earthly kingdom. This choice eventually led to disaster and they were taken in exile to Assyria and later to Babylonia, which is the very symbol of the earthly kingdom. In time a remnant returned and like the days of Moses they went through the wilderness back to rebuild the broken walls and relay the foundations.

These historical stories hold important messages for the church. As we have seen when the church was birthed it walked in a freedom and with power never seen before. Ordinary people did extraordinary things and nothing could stop them. Individuals were set free and on fire as the Spirit of God anointed them with power from on high. They were willing to allow the Spirit to lead and guide and direct their lives and leaders lead by example and their authority came through relationship and servant hood. They were in the world, but not of the world. Then their very success overtook them and when Constantine was baptized, the Christian faith became the official religion of the Roman Empire and it changed the foundations. Within a short time, the church found itself in its own Babylonian exile and outside of the kingdom of God. What seemed like freedom after the years of persecution, became bondage to the control of Levitical priests. On the surface it looked great and many new temples dot the landscape to this day, but God does not live in houses of brick and mortar. Underneath the surface there are many who are tired of seeking the straw to make the bricks to build the expensive earthly sanctuaries to keep the system going. Those who have spiritual eyes see that much of the effort and investment lead to pyramids of power, which are nothing else than monuments to death and there is no life coming out of these, however well dressed and preserved.

As a result, every so often a leader arises to bring freedom to the slaves of the religious system. However, more than often these leaders with a real call and anointing from God seek to lay yet again Levitical foundations, just like Moses did when he stepped out first and killed the Egyptian. Thus, we end up with new style of building representing another Christian franchise, but it does not bring freedom. Just like God allowed Samuel to institute the earthly kingdom model when Israel asked for it and used it, so has he used and blessed the earthly choices we have made through the ages. <u>But this is the third day and our Lord is setting the foundation in order to perfect his body.</u> It is the fulfilment of the words of Jesus in Luke 13:31-35:

> *On that very day some Pharisees came, saying to Him, "Get out and depart from here, for Herod wants to kill you." And He said to them, "Go, tell that fox, <u>'Behold, I cast out demons and perform cures today and tomorrow, and the third day I shall be perfected.' Nevertheless, I must journey</u>*

> *today, tomorrow, and the day following; for it cannot be that*
> *a prophet should perish outside of Jerusalem.*
>
> *"O Jerusalem, Jerusalem, the one who kills the prophets and*
> *stones those who are sent to her! How often I wanted to gather*
> *your children together, as a hen gathers her brood under her*
> *wings, but you were not willing! See! Your house is left to you*
> *desolate; and assuredly, I say to you, you shall not see Me*
> *until the time comes when you say, 'Blessed is He who comes*
> *in the name of the LORD!'" (NKJV).*

In the church through God's grace and mercy we have seen healing and deliverance. These are signs for the first and second day. Now we are moving into the third day and he is setting the stage to bring his body to perfection. He will return for a pure and spotless bride. He is calling forth a remnant to move out of exile and into freedom. He has taken his church past Passover and Pentecost and we are entering the feast of Tabernacles. He is calling forth those who will walk out of the bondage past the gate of fear and intimidation into the wilderness to meet him. He is calling a new generation of deliverers like Moses, to spend time in the wilderness learning to take care of sheep and willing to live in obscurity. He is calling out those who are tired of serving men with titles and robes, even if they have good intentions. He is calling out the No-names willing to pay the price to be perfected and willing to suffer for the kingdom. He is calling those who have seen the truth and are not willing to be buried in the magnificent graves of ecclesiastical pyramids. God is calling his son out of Egypt! Hear his voice:

Come to me, all you who are weary and burdened, and I will give you rest.
Take my yoke upon you and learn from me, for I am gentle and humble in heart,
and you will find rest for your souls.
For my yoke is easy and my burden is light." (Matthew 11:28-30).

"Come, all you who are thirsty, come to the waters;
and you who have no money, come, buy and eat!
Come, buy wine and milk without money and without cost.

Why spend money on what is not bread,
and your labor on what does not satisfy?
Listen, listen to me, and eat what is good,
and your soul will delight in the richest of fare.
Give ear and come to me; hear me, that your soul may live.

I will make an everlasting covenant with you,
my faithful love promised to David.
See, I have made him a witness to the peoples,
a leader and commander of the peoples.
Surely you will summon nations you know not,
and nations that do not know you will hasten to you,

Our Lord is calling those who sense the stirring of this new day in their spirit to come out and tabernacle with him. It is a journey that few in our society have taken, for our focus has been on buildings and structures controlled by Levitical priests running costly programs. Yet it is a journey many in other parts of the world understand very well. It is a journey away from the comfort zones and security to which we have become addicted, into the wilderness of everyday life. It is a journey outside the gate into suffering and persecution. It is a journey into the dry land, which will only be changed as rivers of water flow from our innermost being. It is a journey to a promised land by faith, like the one Abraham took as we read in Hebrews 11:8-10:

By faith Abraham, when called to go to a place he would later receive as his inheritance, obeyed and went, even though he did not know where he was going. By faith he made his home in the Promised Land like a stranger in a foreign country; he lived in tents, as did Isaac and Jacob, who were heirs with him of the same promise. For he was looking forward to the city with foundations, whose architect and builder is God.

It is a journey toward this city where ordinary people become royal priests in the order of Melchizedek and where every day becomes sanctified and where the glory of God is revealed and fills the very place where they gather, even if it is just two or three gathered in his name. It is the journey through the veil into the Most Holy Place and the place where we can enjoy rest and be productive for eternity.

In the introduction I mentioned that this book was not written for the sake of confrontation with those who have a vested interest in the current structures and religious systems. It was written as God's Spirit is moving in the midst of a growing remnant who knows that there is more to our faith than what is being offered to the spiritual consumers in the church marketplace with all its variety. It is written for the many hurting sheep wandering without a shepherd and fearful to enter the fold again. It is written for those who have thought about these things, but have been afraid to step through the gate into what seems to be a wilderness and desert. It is also written for those who have Levitical roots and a vested interest in the status quo, yet know that the old wineskin cannot hold the new wine. Let me encourage you as I remind you of the beginning of the first day! Nearly two thousand years ago a small group of No-names walked through the gate and saw Jesus die on the cross. Soon after that, they were in an upper room and the Holy Spirit empowered them. They walked out into the street and kept going – willing to bear the disgrace of the cross. Some had a vested interest in the structures of the day, for their livelihood depended upon those structures. Yet the Levite, Barnabus, for example left his comfort zone and became an apostle. He literally sold what he owned and gave it to the apostles to meet the needs of the community called the church (Acts 4:36-37). As the No-names continued to do the work of ministry, we read in Acts 6:7:

So the word of God spread. The number of disciples in Jerusalem increased rapidly, and <u>a large number of priests became obedient to the faith.</u>

The same thing is beginning to happen today and the Levitical priesthood and its structures will not last. The church's foundation has as its cornerstone the stone that was rejected by man but chosen by God as precious. His name is Jesus and he was appointed as High Priest in the order of Melchizedek. He was not a Levite. In his blood there is a new covenant and thus the old Levitical covenant with its hierarchy and regulations has become obsolete. In this third day he is perfecting his body and every member will walk in the power and authority of royal priests in the order of Melchizedek. It is time to walk through the gate out of the Babylonian exile and away from the bondage of Egyptian pyramids. <u>Let him who has ears hear his word for today written in Isaiah 43:16-21:</u>

This is what the LORD says--
he who made a way through the sea,
a path through the mighty waters,
who drew out the chariots and horses,
the army and reinforcements together,
and they lay there, never to rise again,
extinguished, snuffed out like a wick:

<u>"Forget the former things;</u>
<u>do not dwell on the past.</u>
<u>See, I am doing a new thing!</u>
<u>Now it springs up;</u>
<u>do you not perceive it?</u>
<u>I am making a way in the desert</u>
<u>and streams in the wasteland.</u>
<u>The wild animals honor me,</u>
<u>the jackals and the owls,</u>
<u>because I provide water in the desert</u>

> *and streams in the wasteland,*
> *to give drink to my people, my chosen,*
> *the people I formed for myself*
> *that they may proclaim my praise."*

ABOUT THE AUTHOR

Dr. Willie Joubert was born in what was known as Tanganyika in East Africa and grew up on a farm that his parents pioneered after World War 2. It was an amazing childhood growing up in amidst wild animals with no hydro, phones, radios or TVs! When he was 11 they moved to a farm in South Africa. Going to school in the nearby town unbeknownst to him at the time was the fact that one of his classmates in Grade 6 would be his future wife.

Following graduation, he attended the University of Pretoria where he completed a Master's degree in Semitic Languages and a degree in Theology and subsequently a Ph.D. in Old Testament Studies. Dr. Joubert taught Semitic Languages for 7 years at the University of Pretoria before he immigrated to Canada with his wife, Eda, and three children. In Canada he pastored in traditional churches as Presbyterian Minister and then in non-denominational settings, worked in church planting as well as in prayer ministry and applying his faith in business settings and in support of para-church ministries. These journeys led to a re-examining of the Biblical foundations of the Church and a conclusion that the future of the church will necessitate a return to the simplicity of the early church in small home-based churches where ordinary people will do the work of ministry.

With this conviction Willie and Eda pioneered a home church and began to network with others. In the process he wrote a number of books and shared the copies with friends and with anyone interested in these. Recently he decided to formally publish these books so that a wider audience can tap into the resources. "Restoring the broken foundations" was the first in a series reflecting their journey of faith and form the foundation to grasp the concept of the Biblical foundations of the church. This book is the next in the series. May it become a blessing to many!